D0012459

RED VELVET UNDERGROUND

CALGARY PUBLIC LIBRARY

MAY   2016

RED VELVET UNDERGROUND

A ROCK MEMOIR, WITH RECIPES

Freda Love Smith

MIDWAY

AN AGATE IMPRINT

CHICAGO

Copyright © 2015 by Freda Love Smith

All rights reserved. No part of this book may be reproduced or transmitted in any form or by any means, electronic or mechanical, including photocopying, recording, or by any information storage and retrieval system, without express written permission from the publisher.

RED VELVET UNDERGROUND
A Rock Memoir, with Recipes
by Freda Love Smith
ISBN-13: 978-1-57284-175-8
ISBN-10: 1-57284-175-3

First printing September, 2015
Printed in the United States.

Author photo on p. 224 by Stacee Sledge

Library of Congress Cataloging-in-Publication Data is on file at the Library of Congress.

Midway is an imprint of Agate Publishing. Agate books are available in bulk at discount prices. For more information, go to agatepublishing.com.

CHAPTER ONE

Daily Bread

I AM MAKING STRAWBERRY SCONES with my son Jonah. Not Jonah at four, rosy cheeks and long eyelashes, or Jonah at seven, outsized front teeth and towhead crew cut, but Jonah at eighteen, scraggly blond mustache and apparent hangover. And yet my heart flutters. It is 10:30, Sunday morning. Jonah has been home for one day from the University of Illinois, where he just completed his freshman year.

He towers over me. I show him how to zest a lemon. He gets the hang of it, producing little ribbons of zest and a bright smell that elevates our little apartment kitchen, with its yellow 1970s linoleum and rusty appliances, to a place of memory and emotion where more is at stake than a tray of scones. Jonah chops strawberries into small pieces. I cut chunks of semi-solid coconut oil into our dry ingredient mixture of flour, baking powder, and salt. I explain to Jonah that the globs of fat are OK, that they will help yield tender scones, and the last thing you want to do when you make scones is over-mix. What you want to do is under-mix. Again, he gets it. In the kitchen, as in most areas of his life, Jonah has always been a fast study—when he wants to be.

During the year before Jonah left for college, we met in the kitchen like this most Sundays for cooking lessons. I wanted to teach him how to cook to help prepare him for adulthood, to make sure the son I was sending out into the world could take care of himself in this basic way. But the lessons were complicated and layered. They were a chance to spend time together, to talk through the major events of that transitional year, and a way to tie Jonah to the family, a little, at the exact moment when those ties were loosening. Now that he is home for the summer, I am worried that he will struggle to find a comfortable dynamic within the confines of family life. After nine months of relative freedom, will it be hard for him to live at home? And what about us—me, his father, Jake, and his little brother, Henry?

I, for one, did not adjust quickly to Jonah's departure for college. I was a wreck. I often caught myself staring into his weirdly clean bedroom feeling alternately empty and freaked out. I hadn't thought I'd have to contend with this cliché. Eventually, I settled into a new family rhythm. I didn't stop missing him. But I grew at home with the change. Now, I can't exactly see what this summer is going to look like or grasp what this new rhythm is going to feel like.

And so, again, as I have done all my life, I look to the kitchen to be more than just a place to make food. I call upon it to be a place where I make sense of things, just as I did as a five-year-old, cutting biscuits with my grandmother while my parents finalized their divorce; as a ten-year-old, making scrambled eggs for my little brother and myself when our mom worked late; as an eighteen-year-old, subsisting on cheap black bean soup while I struggled to find my way in the music business; as a pregnant, macrobiotic twenty-five-year-old with a new lease on life, nourishing myself and in-utero Jonah with brown rice and seaweed; or as a forty-four-year-old, teaching my teenage son how to roast a chicken.

Right when he landed at home yesterday with multiple bags of dirty laundry, I asked Jonah if I could wake him up at 10:00 to make scones together for a Sunday family brunch. "Fine," he said, "if that's what you want for Mother's Day."

I forgot to mention: It is Mother's Day. And yes, of course, I played that card.

Jonah halves and juices our bald lemon, whisks a tablespoonful of the juice into a bowl of coconut milk, and sets the mixture aside to curdle. We line baking sheets with parchment. I think to myself: *Don't bring up summer jobs. Don't say anything. It's Mother's Day. Your son is home. You're making scones . . .*

And then I say, in a cheerful voice that makes me want to smack myself, "So! Any summer job prospects?"

"Umm," he says. "Yeah. My friend works in a doggy daycare, and he might be able to get me a job there. If somebody quits. Maybe."

I silently beat myself back. I want this time with Jonah to help him adjust—to help all of us adjust—to his being home. I will not ruin the day by lecturing him about our money situation or his alarming lack of initiative. I will not scold him about last summer or about the entire school year, about how he has never, ever had a job. I will not say, "When I was your age."

Although, seriously, when I was his age? When I was his age, I lived in an apartment in a city far from home. I knew how to cook, how to balance a checkbook, how to clean a toilet. I'd had many jobs. I'd started a band. Maybe my path to adulthood was too ac-celerated, and maybe that's why I haven't pushed my children to achieve the autonomy that life pushed on me. I wanted my kids to be kids for as long as possible. But in fostering this, I'm sure I've missed some opportunities to encourage their greater independence. When Jonah turned seventeen, it dawned on me that he was one year from adulthood, and I panicked. I had failed, I realized, to prepare my son for the world by not encouraging him more vehemently to get a job, by not leaving him often enough on his own, by not requiring him to share in household chores. I was overwhelmed with regret, and I must admit that this was a major impetus for the cooking lessons. I was looking for redemption.

I am absorbed, briefly, by the task at hand—folding our ingredients together with a rubber spatula. "Gently," I stress to Jonah. God, but he's a good kid. And I adore him beyond reason.

The thing that will drive me crazy this summer is not his late nights, as his coming in after midnight rarely wakes me anymore; or his outrageous food consumption, as I've become accustomed to those vanishing loaves of bread; or even his grubby room and piles of dirty laundry, which stopped being a problem once I decided that they're not *my* problem. The thing that will drive me crazy is the moldering. The way he sits in his room wearing headphones, on Facebook or whatever for hours and hours, seeming to accomplish nothing. What I really need is for him to show some gumption, some spark of enthusiasm and productivity. And I hate to ruin Mother's Day by haranguing him about getting a job. But I have done the math, I have crunched the numbers, and I don't see how we are going to manage his remaining three years of college without his financial contribution. I really need him to earn some money.

I can't explain why, but I have always been able to earn money, though I've never amassed a penny of it. In middle school and high school I babysat, sold greeting cards, and delivered newspapers. The moment I graduated from high school, I stepped into a professional baking position at an excellent bakery in my hometown of Bloomington, Indiana. At The Daily Bread, I trained to make loaves of bread, baguettes, bagels, and pastries. I learned about mixing, kneading, rising, and proofing, and mastered bakery equipment like scales, heavy-duty mixers, and industrial ovens. Some of the skills I acquired were low-tech; The Daily Bread specialized in Pain Brie, a bread which required repeated beating with a Louisville Slugger that was kept leaning against the bakery wall for this sole purpose. Other skills were more refined, like rolling delicate croissant dough into a flat rectangle, covering it with a smooth sheet of cold butter, cutting it into triangles, and rolling it into perfect crescents. It was a summer of new skills. I learned how to wake myself up at 4:00 in the morning and almost took pleasure in stumbling through pre-dawn Bloomington, muttering to myself, "Time to make the donuts."

I learned, also, that good loud music makes light work, and discovered that the music I loved the most was by a band I'd never even heard before that summer: the Velvet Underground. A friend gave me a cassette tape loaded with Velvets songs, and it lived in the bakery, where it accumulated grimy layers of flour and endured repeated plays on the bakery's dilapidated boom box. I loved picking up the Louisville Slugger and beating the Pain Brie in time to the brutal eighth-note piano outro to "Waiting for My Man." I didn't feel like a kid anymore. I was almost seventeen.

Before that summer, I didn't exactly play an instrument, having long ago given up on violin and failed at bass and guitar. But my boyfriend had a drum set in his basement, and the Velvet Underground had a female drummer, the astounding Maureen Tucker, to inspire me. And so I learned something else that summer: a basic drum beat. And all summer long I baked bread, listened to the Velvets, and played that basic beat. Before the summer ended, I'd formed my first band and played my first rock show.

I didn't know it, but I'd created a template for the next twenty-five years of my life. Almost everything would spring from that summer. There would be more baking. There would be more Velvet Underground. There would be more bands, more shows. And there would be more jobs. Many, many, many more jobs.

I've worked in four different bakeries. I've worked in countless restaurants and cafés as a dishwasher, prep cook, barista, waitress, counter person. I've worked at many colleges and universities: Harvard, Indiana University, the Museum School in Boston, Le Cordon Bleu in Chicago, the University of Nottingham, Northwestern University. My duties have nearly run the gamut: adjunct yoga teacher, department administrator, library information assistant, life-drawing model, assistant registrar, English instructor. I have been a canvasser for Greenpeace, an assistant at *Forced Exposure* magazine, a live-in nanny, and a beauty salon receptionist. For one night, in the middle of a bad, broke month, I was a dancer at the Naked i in Boston. I earned my month's rent on that one night and never went—or looked—back.

Jonah uses an oiled quarter-cup measure to scoop dough onto our cookie sheets. It's a trick I learned during one of my bakery jobs. Many of the culinary skills I've passed on to my kids originate from the kitchens where I've worked. I'm glad to have this knowledge, glad that I have worked and learned my whole life. I want the same for Jonah, but I sure hope he never resorts to some of my more desperate moneymaking ventures, and I hope he doesn't end up with a list of jobs as kaleidoscopic as mine. I'd be happier if he ended up like those friends of mine who have done the same work for years, building a livelihood systematically, progressing and advancing in stages, from associate to junior partner to senior partner, from assistant professor to associate professor to full professor, not flailing around randomly like me. I've hopped from one subsistence job to another, I've stopped and started playing music multiple times, and I wonder, still, at middle age, what exactly I want to do with my life. I don't want him to follow my lead. For now, I want him to get one job, just one nice summer job. As soon as possible.

The house smells like warm strawberries. We tidy up the kitchen, make tea, and set the table for our Mother's Day brunch. The scones bake quickly and turn out brown and beautiful. We sit down together: Jake, fair, bespectacled and boyish, and Henry, still faintly cherubic at thirteen, with big blue eyes and a lingering blond curl or two, and Jonah, cute and lanky, still with those long eyelashes—oh but that mustache!—his hangover succumbing to the strong, hot tea. I rein in my fretting, reminiscing heart. I want to be here, not whacking dough in my past or swimming around in Jonah's unknown future, a future I cannot rush him into. I have done what I can for this Sunday morning. I taught my son to zest a lemon, to curdle milk, to under-mix scones.

We pounce on them and gobble them up, every one. It doesn't matter how many times I have baked scones, at home or at work, I am still amazed that our lumpy, unappetizing mess of a dough has yielded such tender, lightly crumbly treats. They may not be perfect, but they are pretty damn spectacular.

Two weeks later, we are trying our hands at bread. I've been growing this crazy idea in my brain that Jonah could be the family bread baker this summer. This lesson is the first step in my cunning plan. Baking bread is a serene activity in this age of the no-knead loaf, not the strenuous event of my baking days gone by. We don't knead or whack or punch the dough but simply chuck the ingredients into a bowl, stir until it comes together, and give it plenty of hours to sit around. It seems terribly millennial, terribly Jonah—minimal elbow grease, weirdly good results.

I turn on the faucet and show him how to test the temperature of the water on the tender underside of his wrist, rather than on his tougher, less-sensitive fingers. Once the dough is mixed, we set it aside to rise and Jonah goes off to his room, clunking his door behind him.

He has been in his room a great deal these past two weeks.

The first Monday he was home, I returned from work that evening to find him in pajamas, eating a sandwich. Maybe it was unrealistic of me to expect him to be out pounding the pavement, distributing résumés, filling in applications, shaking hands and taking names all over Evanston. But, well—pajamas? Before I could form words, Jonah said, "I applied for tons of jobs today."

"Oh," I said, stunned. "That's great honey! Where?"

"A bunch of stuff on Craigslist. Research experiments."

My heart fell.

"And I applied to be a brand ambassador for a cigar company."

Jonah did get chosen to be a research subject for a study at Northwestern. He listened to bleeps for about an hour and a half and earned himself exactly $10. I quickly realized that he simply didn't have a clue about how to look for a job. I started spouting advice at him:

"Look, it's hard to get a job. You need to spend a few hours a day on this, every day. You need to get out there, walk right into businesses. Don't expect them to come to you." I went on. I couldn't stop.

A few days passed, no progress, while I fought my irrational inner fury, but Jonah, when pressed, said—again—"I applied for tons of jobs today." He'd applied to Starbucks, to Whole Foods. This was better than cigar ambassador, and I was heartened, but I didn't share his faith in the whole online application process and more advice gushed out of my mouth. "Really," I said, "there is just no substitute for initiative. You might want to walk over to these places and introduce yourself."

More days passed. Jonah lived from his room by day, went out with his friends at night. I ran out of clichés to spout. And then, thankfully, something came up that took my mind a little off Jonah. Jake got tenure.

Jake had been a professor of media studies at Northwestern University for three years after holding the same title at the University of Nottingham for four years. Months earlier, he'd submitted his case for tenure, and it entered the mysterious, medieval review process, one carefully designed to promote anxiety and insecurity. We tried not to think about it, though it always lurked in the back of our minds. Then, one morning in May, the dean called Jake. "How are you?" she said. "Great," he said. "Well," she said, "you're about to get even better."

Talk about the phone call that changed your life—from career stress and uncertainty to job security forever, in five short minutes.

But that phone call was the distant echo of a decisive moment fifteen years before. Back then, Jake and I had a band together called the Mysteries of Life, and we'd recorded two records on RCA. When the label dropped us, we had to decide—should we stay in the game and hunt for a new record deal? Jonah was four and I was pregnant with Henry. The music business was feeling awfully unsteady for our growing family. Meanwhile, Jake had been slowly finishing his undergraduate degree at Indiana University and becoming increasingly enchanted with academia. He had his eye on a PhD program in communication and culture. It would put our lives on an entirely different track. It would be a long haul, and it would be a gamble.

We made the decision and took the gamble. After years of further education, this gamble took us across the ocean to England, to the one and only job Jake was offered after finishing his PhD (he applied to forty), and then eventually back across the ocean to a top university by a Great Lake. Finally, with a phone call on a spring morning, the gamble paid off. I should have felt satisfied. I should have felt content. But Jonah didn't have a job. Jonah still needed a job.

Selected list of jobs I had while Jake was in graduate school: apartment leasing agent, cover band drummer, songwriter, tarot card reader.

It is time for the next step in our bread lesson. I summon Jonah out of his room. There isn't much to it, but I don't want him to miss any part of the process. We transfer the bread dough to the refrigerator where it needs to sit and chill for at least a few hours. No-knead bread requires little effort but a lot of time. Some things take time. Eight hours to make bread. Fifteen years to become a tenured professor. And how long for a slightly too-laid-back college boy to land a good summer job?

Ten days. It took him exactly ten days. I knew something had shifted when he emerged from his room that tenth morning, showered, bright-eyed, no trace of the unfortunate mustache, wearing a button-down shirt and his jeans without the rips. "I have an interview at Whole Foods!" he said. "In an hour!"

Adrenalin surged through me, I hurled advice at him: "Tell them you love food," I said. "Yeah," said Jonah, "I mentioned that in my cover letter." Wait, what?—*cover letter*? This only slowed me down for a second. "Smile," I instructed him. "Make eye contact."

"Mother," he said, "I think I got this."

He was right. He had it. Before the end of the day he was clicking "accept" on that online application. Why had I been so worried?

The second most fun part of making bread is shaping the loaf. Jonah is right in there, dipping his hands into a bag of flour, "Flour has the best texture," he says. He always says that when we bake, suggesting that he's inherited some kind of baking gene from me, the one that I inherited from my grandmother. He shapes a reasonably smooth, oblong loaf. After its final rising, he brushes the loaf with water, slashes it with a serrated knife, sprinkles it with salt and seeds, and chucks it into a very hot oven. He sets the timer for thirty minutes. "Hey," says Jonah, "do you want to hear the song I've been working on?" Sometimes I forget that Jonah is a musician because he works on his computer and keyboard with headphones, and nary a peep escapes through the door of his room. When I practiced my drums, people next door knew it, let me tell you.

He plays me the track—a floaty, layered collage with a pretty melody and heavy groove. He has been doing more in his room than I realized. We are so different, Jonah and I. And so alike. I suggest that he jot down our bread recipe. "I was thinking," I say, "maybe you could get this bread-making thing down, and you could make bread for the family while you're here this summer. And, you know, it's a great thing to be able to do, you can wow your roommates someday." Something crosses his face. "Yeah," he says, "that *would* actually be cool. I'll be bread man. OK."

The most fun part of making bread is eating it warm out of the oven. When I worked at The Daily Bread, I celebrated the end of every rigorous morning shift by devouring a warm hunk of bread topped by a melting knob of butter. It made everything worth-while—the hard work, the sleep deprivation, the burnt wrists. It made everything good.

I call the family to our dining table. It's not mealtime; it's just bread time. We sit with thick slices, we pass the butter. Jonah has a job. Jake has tenure. "Jeez," says Jonah, "this is so good. It's like real bread." We all agree, our mouths full. "And it was so *easy!*" he adds.

Easy. For a heavy instant, I feel the crush of time. I feel the hours, the weeks, the years, and I feel the weight of all the troubles I have protected my children from bearing. People argue passion-ately about whether parenting is a profession in itself, whether being a mom or dad is a job. I don't know. It is work I have been doing for nearly nineteen years, and it is the hardest thing I've ever tried to do. It is also, at moments that catch me off guard, as satisfying as anything I've ever tried to do. Sometimes, for just a few moments, for just a few bites of bread, it even feels easy.

"Yeah," I say to Jonah. "Easiest thing in the world."

Vegan Strawberry–Cream Scones

Makes 8

2 cups all-purpose unbleached flour

⅓ cup granulated sugar

2 teaspoons baking powder

½ teaspoon salt

Zest of 1 lemon

1 tablespoon fresh lemon juice

⅔ cup unsweetened, full-fat coconut milk

⅓ cup coconut oil

1 teaspoon vanilla extract

1 cup chopped strawberries (raspberries substitute very well)

1. Preheat the oven to 425°F. Line 2 baking sheets with parchment paper and set aside.

2. In a medium bowl, whisk together the flour, sugar, baking powder, and salt. Stir in the lemon zest. Set aside.

3. In a small bowl, whisk together the lemon juice and coconut milk and set aside to curdle for 1 to 2 minutes. (Put the rest of your fresh lemon juice in your tea or water and drink it; it's supposed to be good for hangovers. Curb your urge to bring up unpleasant topics.)

4. Add the coconut oil to the dry ingredients in globs. Stir with a fork, and use your fingers to gently work the coconut oil into the flour, but go easy—it's fine and good to leave some bigger hunks of fat in there. If you want you can do this in a food processor—just a half-dozen pulses will do the trick.

RECIPE CONTINUES

5.   Add the vanilla to the coconut-milk mixture and stir to combine. Add the wet ingredients to dry ingredients and stir briefly to just combine. Don't beat the hell out of it; you're not looking for smooth perfection, but a roughly combined, lumpy mess. Gently fold in the strawberries (or raspberries).

6.   Using a lightly oiled ¼-cup measure, scoop the batter onto the prepared baking sheets. Keep a couple of inches of space between each scoop. Bake 15 minutes, or until lightly browned. Let cool 1 to 2 minutes on the baking sheets, then transfer to wire racks to cool for a few more minutes.

7.   Serve warm for Mother's Day, or any day.

White Whole-Wheat Bread

Adapted from the Master Recipe in *Healthy Bread in Five Minutes a Day*, by Jeff Hertzberg and Zoë François.

Makes 2 loaves—we usually bake one right away, and one later

3¾ cups white whole-wheat flour

1¼-ounce packet active dry yeast

2 tablespoons vital wheat gluten

2 teaspoons sea salt, plus more for sprinkling

2 cups warm water (slightly warmer than body temperature—test on your wrist)

2 tablespoons sunflower seeds or chopped pumpkin seeds

To Prepare the Dough

1. In a large bowl, whisk together the flour, yeast, wheat gluten, and salt. Using a wooden spoon, stir in the water—you might need to use your hands to incorporate the water—but don't knead. Just work in all the water until the dough is uniform. It will be a fairly wet dough. Loosely cover the bowl with plastic wrap and set aside to rise for 2 hours.

2. Transfer the dough to the refrigerator and chill for at least 3 hours, up to overnight.

To Bake

1. Oil a baking sheet. Set aside.

2. Lightly dust the dough with flour. Halve the dough—you can use a serrated knife. (The unused ½ of the dough can be returned to the fridge, in the same bowl, covered with plastic wrap, and used anytime in the next 14 days.)

RECIPE CONTINUES

3. Add a little more flour to the dough you're working with, so it won't stick to your hands, and form a slightly flattened ball by stretching the dough around to the bottom on all sides, forming a seam on the bottom. Elongate the ball into an oval by gently stretching it. Important: this whole process should take less than 1 minute; try not to over-handle the dough.

4. Place the ball onto the prepared baking sheet and loosely cover with plastic wrap. Let rest for 90 minutes.

5. Preheat the oven to 450°F for at least 20 minutes.

6. In a metal pan, place 1 cup of water. Set the pan on the bottom rack of your oven.

7. Remove the plastic wrap from the dough. Using a pastry brush, paint the loaf with water. Using a serrated knife, slash ¼-inch-deep parallel cuts across the top of the loaf. Sprinkle with the seeds and a few pinches of salt.

8. Bake for 30 minutes. Let cool on a wire rack for a full 30 minutes. Eat. Be happy.

NOTE: If you have a stand mixer, you can prepare the dough in a snap. Whisk the dry ingredients together in the stand mixer bowl, then use the paddle attachment to work the water in. You can keep the dough in the same bowl, cover with plastic wrap, let it rise, and then refrigerate.

CHAPTER TWO

The Summer of Meat and Potatoes

"HERB CHICKENS SELL as soon as we put them out, so it's total luck if you see one of those. If you do, grab it. They are so good."

My son Jonah is an expert on Whole Foods's rotisserie chickens. One of the main duties at his summer job is chicken-making, and he does hundreds of them a day. It sounds like a grisly scene to me, but I am intensely enjoying this conversation.

"Organic chickens, you do not want to buy those in the evening. We make them first thing in the morning because the rules for organic are really specific and strict. It gets too busy during the day to do it right. So we make a bunch of them early in the morning and keep them warm all day. The one you buy at 5:00 has been sitting there since 8:00 in the morning."

Jonah has been working at Whole Foods for a month—washing dishes, sanitizing equipment, making tortilla chips and vats of guacamole and salsa, and preparing lots and lots of chickens. The work is hard and he doesn't love it. He often comes home in the evening too tired to go out with his friends. My heart breaks a little to see him worn out and beaten up, initiated into the drudgery of entry-level food service. It's a transition into the real world of toil and trouble. I didn't expect these flashes of regret at my son's expulsion from his Eden of playing, studying, socializing, and moldering. Would it have been easier if he'd had a job in high school, less of a shock if he'd eased into this reality earlier? Yes, maybe.

Although Jonah seems exhausted by his full-time hours and somewhat shell-shocked by this new reality, I also detect a new self-confidence in him, a spark of grown-up-ness that he sports proudly. Now that I like. It looks good on a nineteen-year-old. And this chicken spiel is really pretty delightful.

"Now the Cajun spice, that's a no. Just—no."

"Isn't it funny," I say, "that your first job is making chickens, and the first thing I ever taught you how to cook was roasted chicken?"

Jonah says he remembers. And of course he does. It wasn't that long ago, just a little over two years. Barely a blip to me. Forty-three, forty-five, what's the difference? But seventeen to nineteen, that's a big leap.

Actually, Jonah was only sixteen when we started our series of cooking lessons, which ended up spanning a little over a year. His seventeenth birthday was two weeks away. Maybe it's because our family has gone through so many relocations and reinventions, maybe that's why I rely intensely on birthdays to mark time, to help me keep my history straight. Whenever one of my children's birthdays approaches, I dive into introspective time travel. Jonah's approaching milestone was shaking me up, bringing up more than the usual nostalgia.

How could it have been seventeen years since that hot June afternoon, that long, mellow homebirth, and Jonah's arrival as a gorgeous, nine-pound peach of a baby, with big, clear blue eyes? Jake and I were in our twenties, too young, totally blissed out and excited, but with no clue as to what we were getting ourselves into. No clue that, exactly one year later, we would find ourselves exhausted but deeply in love with Jonah and flush with joy and pride when our little birthday boy deliberately stood up, took one perfect step, his first ever, and sat down again, cross legged and content. As if he knew it was his first birthday. As if he'd read the baby development books and knew the drill. I was thrilled and ran out to buy him a birthday present: his first pair of shoes, tiny Converse sneakers to outfit his exit from babyhood to toddlerhood.

Of course, we also had no clue as to how disorienting and exhilarating it would be to parent a teenager. Before that seventeenth birthday, it felt like we were hovering at a pivotal moment— our oldest son's final year of high school imminent, his plans for college and beyond a murky unknown. All sentimental reminiscing aside, what was hitting me the hardest was the reality of Jonah's approaching future.

He didn't know what he wanted to study, where he wanted to study, what he wanted to *be*. Academic success came easily to Jonah—his test scores were high, his grades were good—but no subject set him on fire. He muttered about a gap year, but without any plan or conviction.

I wasn't much different when I was his age. I'd dropped out of Indiana University when I was seventeen, with the sensible career plan of being a rock drummer. I didn't take a gap year, I took two gap decades. Twenty years, many bands, and two babies later, I returned to college and earned a degree in my mid-thirties. I was no role model for Jonah. I'd had some intermittent success in music, and I'd recently completed a master's degree in creative writing, but for the most part my educational history was as fraught as my career history. In fact, as Jonah's birthday and senior year approached, I had just found out I was losing my job as an adjunct English teacher at a culinary arts college, and the best thing I'd been able to line up was a temporary administrative job at Northwestern, where Jake was a newly hired professor. Maybe it was unfair of me to expect Jonah to have some kind of a clear and focused plan for college and beyond. But I have always hoped to steer him away from the messy roads I've travelled.

Besides, it was 2010 and we were in an era of economic downturn and massive unemployment, with the threat of a double-dip recession looming large. I couldn't help being just plain worried about the kid's prospects. And like most parents of teenagers, I was eager for signs of enthusiasm about something. Anything. I wanted him to be a person who was really into something, and I didn't care what. The happiest people I know are those most deeply involved in what they do, obsessed with something, whether it's with mastering the upright bass, baking the perfect biscuit, hiking the Pacific Crest Trail, programming a killer drumbeat, or knitting an incredible pair of wool socks.

What did I think it would accomplish, teaching my son to cook? I didn't expect that it would help him settle on a college or a line of work. I didn't think it would make up for my example. Part of it was simple: He was leaving home, theoretically, in a year, and I wanted him to depart with this fundamental skill. That was enough of a reason. But there was more. There was terror, for one thing—the kind of terror that hits when you feel the years sneak by. There was a need to find a place of connection, to have longer conversations with my son and to get him out of his room. And there was my need to acknowledge the significance of that year ahead, a year that would, possibly, end with his departure for college, marking the end of his childhood.

Cooking lessons were my best idea for dealing with this overwhelming host of feelings and circumstances. I wrapped a lot up into the idea, which had been evolving in the back of my head for a while, and I'd proposed it to Jonah a few months earlier. I knew that if he said no there would be no recourse. Forcing your kid into a year of cooking lessons would be sheer hell.

But he hadn't said no. Maybe this was a little uncharacteristic of your average sixteen-year-old, and for this willingness I can thank Jonah's lifelong love of food. Though I have already complained about his general lack of enthusiasm, I must admit this was unfair—Jonah has *always* been enthusiastic about food. Maybe it's partly a genetic inheritance, but I have to think it's mostly inspired by the unique circumstances of his childhood.

I like the saying that every baby comes with a loaf of bread under its arm. Jonah came with a record contract. When I became pregnant with him, Jake and I were still eking out a living in the indie rock band Antenna. A baby, we decided, would put a stop to all of that, so we quit the band and started looking for jobs and re-enrolling in college. Jonah was born and we were plugging away at our new civilian life, playing and recording quiet music in our living room, just for fun, in a new band we dubbed the Mysteries of Life. But when a friend sent some of those living room recordings out into the world, we were surprised to find ourselves diving back into music, signing a recording contract with RCA.

But how to manage that dive with a little one? We made it up as we went along, renting an RV, hiring a friend as a nanny, and embarking on a family rock and roll adventure. Jonah spent a lot of time on tour when he was one and two years old, and he got used to eating in restaurants every night. He learned how to eat anything. Band mates watched, amazed, as little Jonah gobbled up nori rolls coated in fish eggs or black bean burritos with hot salsa.

Touring, eating out, and staying in hotels were deeply formative experiences for him, demonstrated by his habit in preschool of picking up the toy phone and ordering room service ("Stwawbe- wwies," he would command down the plastic receiver. "Scwam- bled eggs") and by the fact that even today he can sleep anywhere. Jonah was a fun kid to feed, on tour and at home, where I cooked him kale, brown rice, butternut squash, tofu, lentil soup, and sea- weed, along with the standard macaroni and cheese, broccoli, and spaghetti. Jonah ate it all. He ate everything.

By the time he was twelve, our music career had sputtered out, and our family moved from our hometown of Bloomington, Indiana, to Nottingham, England, a small city in the East Mid- lands, where Jake had landed his first academic job. During our four years in England, we travelled as often as we could manage, affording Jonah the opportunity to further expand his adven- turous eating habits. He devoured a plate of snails in Paris, tiny sardines—skin, bones, and all—in Turkey, and regularly cleaned his plate of the East Midlands specialty, mushy peas, which I could never bring myself to try. Jonah's brother, Henry, five years his junior, has always been a more typical kid with food, a rather picky eater who takes the onions out of his spaghetti sauce and for years refused to eat either mushrooms or any kind of soup. ("It's not soup," I would insist, "it's *bisque*." He didn't buy it. He was picky—not stupid.)

Jonah is into food. "Great meal," is his standard line after almost every meal. So it wasn't really a surprise, then, when he agreed to my cooking lesson idea. He had one of those hearts that you reach via stomach, and when you love to eat it's only natural to want to learn to cook. Maybe there was more to it for Jonah, too. Maybe he was glad for an excuse to spend a little more time in the family fold, to find a comfortable space at home right as his realm was extending far beyond the household. I missed him. Maybe he missed me too, just a little.

Whatever the reasons, I was delighted that this was going to happen. I had proposed the cooking lessons in the spring, and we had a few months to plan. I had stressed the collaborative nature of the project from the start, running all of my ideas by Jonah, testing recipes on the family as we geared up to start. As a gesture of goodwill, I suggested that we launch the cooking lessons with meat-based meals. Jonah leapt at this.

I have been mostly vegetarian for most of my life, and at home I cook almost entirely veggie, with the occasional piece of fish thrown in. Yet somehow I'd raised a devoted carnivore, like the stereotypical hippie parents whose kids rebel by joining the Young Republicans. I knew Jonah would get excited about cooking meat. The boundaries were shifting at home in this regard, anyway. Henry, previously a staunch vegetarian, had renounced and become a meat-eater again—"I couldn't take it anymore," he'd said, although in a year he'd be back on the vegetarian wagon. While Henry has always swung from one extreme to another, I have always hovered in a wishy-washy, kinda-sorta territory. I hadn't eaten a roast chicken in years. But I was craving it. I'd walk by those rotisserie chickens in Whole Foods, the ones that Jonah would later be cranking out en masse, and the smell brought out the animal in me. And so the cooking lessons began, one Sunday afternoon in early June, with roasted chicken and vegetables.

For all Jonah's carnivorous ways, I still wasn't sure how he'd respond to the veiny, pink, slippery reality of a raw chicken. When I slapped it into the kitchen sink, he did shudder, slightly. "Beautiful," he said. I wondered, too, if my salmonella speech would put him off. Wash your hands, wash your surfaces, wash your tools. Meat is really somewhat off-putting in its uncooked state. For all the many, many hours of my life I've spent in one kitchen or another, I have spent very little time cooking animals and have always felt that cooking vegetables is so much simpler and cleaner.

But after that initial shudder, Jonah wasn't even slightly squeamish and was soon handling the chicken with ease, flipping it around in his hands and rubbing it with salt, pepper, olive oil, and thyme. I knew Jonah would appreciate how truly simple it is to make a chicken dinner, and he did. He couldn't believe there wasn't more to it. I gave him a couple of knives to try—a small, well-sharpened paring knife and my favorite trusty old Caddie, a Japanese chef knife that's been with me for years. Armed with the Caddie, he chopped our vegetables, fumbling a bit at first—too tentative in the manner of a new cook but quickly becoming more confident and competent. He took to the kitchen. At Le Cordon Bleu, the culinary college where I taught English, the students spend their entire first term developing knife skills, learning how to cut, slice, chop, mince, and dice. Jonah loved this—I think it sounded like more fun than his AP History class. "Maybe I'll go to cooking school!" he said, gleefully waving the Caddie around, whacking up the carrots with a little more flair.

We piled the vegetables around the chicken, and into the oven it went. Meat was a good place to start. It helped Jonah get excited about cooking lessons and set this meal apart from our typical rice and beans fare. Moreover, the prep work is a snap, and the odds for success and satisfaction are very high. Meat is easy.

Satisfied was exactly how I'd describe my son when he removed the pan from the oven to a picture-perfect golden chicken surrounded by heaps of browned, roasted veggies. Jonah whipped out his phone and took a picture, clearly pleased with himself.

Satisfied is also how I'd describe our family as we devoured that feast and how I'd describe myself after cooking lesson number one came to a happy conclusion. Good start. It was a very good start.

Two weeks after the launch of cooking lessons, and being in the kitchen with Jonah already felt normal. The day after our first dinner we'd made chicken salad with the leftover meat, and then we'd made soup with the bones, which gave me a chance to feel like an old-time home-economics teacher, giving Jonah a lesson in thrift. I figure if you're going to eat an animal, don't waste any of it. He agreed, and the results were delicious. But for Jonah's seventeenth birthday, we went for a major splurge: grass-fed sirloin steak. It cost a fortune. I was not crazy about cooking cow, and steak would not tempt me like roast chicken did. But it was Jonah's birthday, and it was his unequivocal first choice.

I wondered if there was some kind of link between Jonah's meat-loving and my prenatal diet, which was almost entirely vegan and macrobiotic. It was a healthy pregnancy, but I was alarmed to find out, midway through, that my iron levels were extremely low. "Could you eat a steak or two?" asked my midwife, who didn't trust my vegetarian ways. The moment she asked, I knew the answer was yes. Steak, suddenly, sounded good. I ate a few of them, upped my intake of vegetarian iron sources, and soon my levels were nice and high and my meat-eating days were mostly over, for the time being. Could those few well-placed steaks that improved my health during his gestation have somehow influenced Jonah to love meat, steak in particular? Probably not, but seeing as how he was the product of mostly vegetables, I've always wondered.

I had been thinking about Jonah's first birthday gift, those little Converse sneakers, as I pondered what to get him for his seventeenth. I settled on a good chef knife—a handy tool and an appropriate symbol. He was sincerely pleased. "Great," he said, teasing me, "now I have my own knife. I can join a street gang." Funny, coming from a kid who'd never been in trouble in his life.

There was no rumbling and no fuss at all as we cooked Jonah's expensive but simple birthday dinner. It was a total caveman meal, meat on flame. He'd requested asparagus as a side, and this we quick-boiled in salted water. I explained to Jonah how transferable this all was, that most vegetables and any kind of steak can be made with the techniques we were using. Jonah was quick, enthusiastic, happy with his new knife, and rapturous (as were Henry and Jake) over the food.

As our family ate that birthday dinner, Jonah made an announcement: He had a girlfriend. His first. My heart did actually skip a beat. I'd been wondering when Jonah would enter the world of romance, and wasn't it so like him to announce this milestone on his birthday? We bombarded him with questions, who/what/when/where/how, and then I just asked, "Are you happy?"

"Super happy," he replied, and he radiated something that was very new indeed. I made a mental note—time to initiate a sex talk. A real one. Not the abstract, philosophical one, but the do-not-get-an-STD-or-make-a-baby one. Not at the dinner table, though.

I wish I could suspend Jonah's seventeenth birthday at that fluttery, cheerful dinner table. But the day was going to change in tone, big time, in just a few hours with an unwelcome phone call.

Jake and I had settled down later that night, cold beers in hand, to watch a cop show about a missing teenage girl who'd had a secretive, complicated life. I actually felt a twinge of smug satisfaction about my reasonably well-adjusted, healthy boys. Smugness, of course, is always a red flag.

The phone rang. I picked it up.

"Hi?" said Jonah.

I knew something was wrong. He'd only left the house forty-five minutes earlier to meet his girlfriend and some friends. He wasn't due home for hours.

"Oh my God, what?" I said.

"There's been some trouble," he said, relaxed and collected as always. "The police are here. I need you to come pick me up."

"The *what*?" I said. "What?"

Jake took the phone out of my hands. Minutes later, he stormed off. I sat in shock, biting my nails, drinking my beer, and thirty minutes later Jake slammed the door and ordered Jonah, who tried to slink off to his room, to sit next to me and tell me the story.

He told the story, infuriatingly calm. He'd been riding in a carful of teenagers (breaking one law right off the bat by the sheer number of bodies piled into the car), when the police pulled them over and searched the car. They found a few cans of beer, a bottle of booze, and a Sucrets tin of pot. None of the teens were high or drunk, but it was clear that had the police pulled them over an hour or so later it would have been a different story. Jonah easily could have spent his seventeenth birthday night sitting in the police station or a jail cell. But the cops had mercy and asked the kids to call home instead, leaving the consequences up to each family.

What would those consequences be? I couldn't even think of how to respond to this shockingly stupid situation. And I couldn't help but go crashing back to my own adolescence in Bloomington, all the reckless nights I survived, my parents blissfully unaware. Bloomington is and was a raging college town, a place where you can always find a party if you know where to look. I knew. I drank every horrible thing you can think of: crappy keg beer, peppermint schnapps, Everclear, Long Island iced tea. I smoked clove cigarettes, menthol cigarettes, tried hash, tried pot, and often relied on cheap speed or diet pills to make it through the more trying days of high school.

Who was I to judge Jonah? Just as I'd been wondering when romance and sex were going to matter more to Jonah, I'd wondered if intoxicants were a factor in his life. I couldn't help but worry when he clunked in late, thrashed around in the kitchen, slammed into his room. I'd often get out of bed on those nights, stand in the kitchen doorway, watch him make a sandwich, and try to make conversation. He never had much to say, and his eyes did appear a little bleary sometimes. But he never missed curfew, never got sick, never missed a day of school or even a class.

And what about me? I missed school often enough to be on a very close first-name basis with the truant officer. I was sick often. My drinking habits would eventually lead me to some truly dangerous situations—blacked out on the floor of a stranger's bathroom or hauled out of the Rathskeller, a bar in Boston, by three bouncers, tossed into the alley on account of underage drinking while I screamed, "Break my legs!" My friend Adam stayed by my side, watching the bouncers carefully. "Don't break her legs, please," he said politely. That dumb incident resulted in my band, the Blake Babies—still relatively new at the time and trying to make our way on the Boston scene—getting slapped with a one-year ban on playing in one of the city's crucial venues. Everybody played at the Rat—the Pixies, the Throwing Muses, Galaxie 500, Christmas, the Lemonheads. But not the Blake Babies, not for a whole year, thanks to me. I'd dared to venture back once during that ban, armed with a fake ID, a long black wig, and a face covered in make-up to see my favorite band at the time, the Volcano Suns. It was an incredibly stupid move. (Although they were a great band.)

It was probably for the best that I eventually landed in the hospital with alcohol poisoning, and the doctors fast-tracked me into rehab where I went through days of painful withdrawal followed by a couple of reasonably happy and stable years in Alcoholics Anonymous. Jonah had a long way to go to even approach my lack of good judgment.

But I never had a single run-in with the cops. My parents never got one of these phone calls. I was worse than Jonah. I am sure of it. I was just better at not getting caught. But I wondered: does that mean I'm not allowed to be angry, not allowed to lecture my son, not allowed to punish him? Is being a hypocrite an inescapable part of parenting a teen?

I couldn't sort all this out. I was exhausted. True to form, Jonah had saved every coming-of-age milestone for the day of his

birthday. He'd taken a big step into some new and dangerous territory. Not only did we have to have the real-life sex talk, we also
had to have the real-life drugs and alcohol talk.

And the kid who'd never been in trouble was grounded for the
first time in his life.

Food was one of the thin shreds of fabric holding our family together for the rest of that summer. Everything swirled into chaos.
After less than a year living back in the states, we had to leave
our temporary housing and find a new apartment in Evanston.
Amidst the packing and moving, I blundered through the early
days of my new job as an administrative temp at Northwestern.
At the same time, my paternal grandmother, Violet, fell gravely
ill, taking a turn for the worse after years of slow decline due to
leukemia. I flew to Tennessee to say goodbye.

Through it all, we had to eat, and the cooking lessons marched
on. Father's Day happened to fall during the week that Jonah was
grounded. It was such a strange week, all of us shaken up, not sure
exactly how to act. Jonah in particular was quieter than I'd ever
seen him. Cooking helped. Jonah and I concocted a festive Father's Day menu: barbecue chicken with a homemade spice rub
and creamy potato salad. That meal was by far the happiest and
most cohesive moment of that uncomfortable week and proved
without a doubt that it's hard to be depressed while licking barbecue sauce off your fingers.

We had another meaty feast soon after moving into our new
home. We hadn't wanted to move, but the new place was sweet—a
vintage apartment organized around a long hallway with a huge
living room and dining room, a working fireplace, and pretty
built-in shelves. Beyond these expansive common rooms there
were three small bedrooms and a narrow, outdated kitchen with
small, bright yellow 1970s counters and fake wood-paneled cabi-
nets. I would miss the big modern kitchen of our university condo.

On the bright side, the old place had an electric range and oven that I could never get used to, and I loved the gas stove in the new place. The new kitchen also had a few cute details that redeemed it, like an arched cutout window between the kitchen and Jake's small office ("You can hand me plates of cookies through here," Jake explained, only pretending to be kidding), and a good-sized pantry with a high shelf that the owners had built to hold a radio. I loved the high ceiling, too, and the whole apartment had such a great feel to it that it was easy to forgive its shortcomings.

Honestly, though, for all my fond feelings about it, I had one single overriding impression when I surveyed our quirky new apartment full of the mostly crappy cheap furniture that we'd accumulated: We were living like graduate students. We had jobs at a good university, and our kids were in middle school and high school. I'd imagined that by this stage of life we'd be in a bigger house with prettier furniture. We'd done a good job of getting ourselves educated and employed, and we'd taken good care of our kids, but we'd done a lousy job of managing our money. We'd borrowed way too much in student loans and lost money on the first house we'd bought when its value plummeted the year we really had to sell it. We'd fallen hard off the property ladder. I didn't know if we'd ever climb back on. This apartment was the best we could hope for right then.

We broke in our funny little kitchen by making meatloaf. Maybe not the obvious choice for a ninety-degree day (and no air conditioning), and making meatloaf takes some serious elbow grease, too. We worked up a sweat, reminiscent of beating the Pain Brie in my baker days or pounding through a summer gig in my drumming days. It was good, though, and a big novelty—we are definitely not a meatloaf kind of family. I'd eaten plenty of meatloaf growing up but never made it myself until we'd lived in England. A family friend, Henry's teacher Mr. Bumstead, cheerfully invited himself over for dinner one day and requested that I make meatloaf—Mr. Bumstead had been served meatloaf during a visit to the US and it was his favorite American food. I couldn't possibly say no, so I worked out a decent meatloaf recipe, and Mr. Bumstead was pleased enough with it to invite himself over on a regular basis. My version of meatloaf is different from my mom's—a bit zingier and baked with mashed potatoes piled on top. Maybe this would have been a better lesson for the winter, as it really wasn't summer food, but everybody loved it and the leftovers gave Jonah a new ingredient for his late-night sandwiches.

Once he was no longer grounded, there were longer gaps between our cooking lessons. Jonah spent less time at home, more time out with his girlfriend and friends. He went away for a few days to a music festival in Michigan where he camped out with his friends and—to my delight—cooked his meals on a camp stove. Meat on flame, he was getting it! During that same time, Henry was off at camp, leaving Jake and me in a temporarily empty nest. It was a strange, quiet period, a disorienting taste of days to come. It didn't seem possible that Jonah would be going away to college in only a year. I certainly couldn't imagine the days when he'd be home after a successful first year of college, working his butt off at Whole Foods, handing out advice about the relative merits of organic versus herb chickens. So much needed to happen to Jonah. I wasn't sure if it was happening or not.

Finally, the summer just crashed completely down on me. My sweet grandmother died, and nothing had prepared me for the loss. A few days later, Jake and I collapsed into bed at 10:30 when our apartment buzzer sounded. Something was wrong.

It was Jonah, buzzing because he had no house key and no phone. Both had been stolen. He and a friend had been mugged by four men on an unlit Evanston street. He was calm. *What,* I wondered, *will ever ruffle this kid?* We called the police, who arrived minutes later, and there we were, in our barely unpacked living room, embroiled in our second interaction with the Evanston police that summer. As scary as his teenage car bust had been, this was scarier. The helplessness and vulnerability I felt after he was mugged shook me to my motherly core. It drove home the awful truth: I had very little power to protect this child. I told myself that it could have been worse. Like everything else that summer.

I tumbled into a shaking depression that lasted weeks. It didn't help that my new temp job was stressful and wearing. I was earning a paycheck but my wheels were spinning—I wasn't on track to a promising future any more than Jonah was. And, to crown that miserable period, I became really sick with a nasty cough that wouldn't go away. It was during this time that I suggested to Jonah he take his first solo flight in the kitchen. Maybe dinner would help. Maybe Jonah cooking dinner for me would help.

He agreed readily and chose roast chicken—no surprise there. I picked up the ingredients on my way home from work, gave him a few suggestions and reminders, then willingly allowed myself to be banned from the kitchen. I curled up in bed with a book and a cup of tea. In bed! While my son made dinner for the family. At one point I yelled in from my room, asking if he needed any help.

"I'm fine," he said. "I'll tell you if I need you."

He didn't need me. And that was fine.

The house smelled amazing, and then there we were, sitting around Jonah's meal. I ate. Without the slightest pang of vegetarian guilt I ate and loved every bite. It was perfect. The trials of the summer fell away: the police reports and worries, the sickbed and the deathbed, the moving truck and job stress. All of that evaporated, just for a while, beneath a platter of food on a table for four. The dinner table had been, more than once that summer, a place of refuge, a place to reconnect and recover. That night, it felt like even more. It felt like a place to celebrate the things that were going right. I'd forgotten, I think, that anything was going right. A happy marriage, two great kids, food on the table! Plenty was right.

For years, ever since the boys were very little, we've had a family ritual at the dinner table called "the two-thing game." The rules are simple: each family member shares two things about his or her day, such as something weird or interesting that happened, some realization or lesson learned, or just a good joke. We played the two-thing game that night, and when it was Jonah's turn he announced that he wanted to try being vegan for a month. Wow, I hadn't seen that one coming. But I celebrated this surprise announcement. Jonah was thinking about food; he was curious to explore different ways of cooking and eating. And I would be on surer footing with plant-based meals. There seemed to be some kind of symmetry to this, too, as the decadent and dramatic summer of meat and potatoes gave way to the austere autumn of lentils and beans. I was ready for less drama, and perhaps some simple, peaceful meals would accompany some simple, peaceful days. This was a welcome thought. Maybe I'd get some peace, maybe I wouldn't, but I couldn't complain about anything in that moment. The summer ended on a sweet, high note.

I couldn't have seen what Jonah would be like two years later. Here he is, preparing to start his sophomore year in college, his major declared, his path taking shape, waking up at the crack of dawn to cook hundreds of chickens for ten dollars an hour, giving me advice, teaching me a thing or two. He still has a lot to learn. Don't we all?

"Your best bet at Whole Foods is a plain, roasted chicken. Those chickens had a good life. And we cook them all day."

"Glad to know it," I say. And I am.

Roast Chicken and Vegetables

The only comment from my tester on this one was, "Oh my God, so fucking good!"

Serves 4

1 lemon, halved

4 medium carrots, cut into ½-inch chunks

4 medium potatoes, peeled and cut into ½-inch chunks

½ cup olive oil, divided

2 tablespoons fresh thyme leaves (stems removed and discarded), divided

2 teaspoons salt, divided

1 teaspoon freshly ground black pepper, divided

1 3½-pound roasting chicken, giblets removed, rinsed and patted dry

1. Preheat the oven to 500°F.

2. In a small bowl, juice the lemon and set aside. Reserve the lemon halves.

3. In a large bowl, combine the veggies with ¼ cup of the olive oil, 1 tablespoon of the thyme, 1 teaspoon of the salt, and ½ teaspoon of the black pepper. Pour the mixture into a roasting pan and evenly spread it out.

4. In the same large bowl, combine the remaining ¼ cup of the oil, 1 tablespoon of the thyme, 1 teaspoon of the salt, and ½ teaspoon of the pepper. Add the lemon juice and whisk well. Plop in the chicken, turning it over and around with your hands to coat with the mixture. Transfer the chicken to the roasting pan on top of the vegetables, stuff the lemon halves into the chicken, and bake for 20 minutes.

5.   After 20 minutes, reduce the oven temperature to 375°F and bake for 40 more minutes (you can baste it every now and then if you like), or until the skin is brown and a little crispy, and a thermometer stuck into the joint of the thigh and drumstick reads 160°F.

6.   Remove from the oven, loosely cover with foil, and let rest for 5 minutes before carving—this gives the juices that have been pushed to the surface by the heat of the oven a chance to be re-absorbed, resulting in much juicier meat.

NOTE: If you want to make Chicken Noodle Soup (page 36) after eating the chicken (believe me, you do!), then try to save some meat—get in there and pull all of it off the bones, ideally 1–2 cups' worth. Store tightly covered. Save the bones and goo, too—don't throw anything away, just put it all (separate from the meat) in a resealable container and refrigerate.

Chicken Noodle Soup

This is what everybody in my family wants when they're sick. If I just want soup and don't have a leftover chicken on hand, I'll make this with a store-bought rotisserie chicken.

Serves 6–8

6 stalks celery, divided

6 carrots, peeled, divided

Bones from 1 roast chicken

1 medium onion, peeled and halved

3–4 cloves garlic, peeled and halved

2 dried bay leaves

1 teaspoon salt, plus more to taste

½ teaspoon ground turmeric

½ teaspoon dried thyme

¼ teaspoon ground white pepper

¼ teaspoon ground cayenne pepper, optional

8 ounces egg noodles or orzo pasta

1–2 cups leftover chicken, or whatever you've got,
    chopped into small pieces

1. Chop 4 of the celery stalks and 4 of the carrots. Set aside.

2. In a large soup pot, combine the bones, onion, garlic, the 2 whole celery stalks and 2 whole carrots, and the bay leaves. Cover with 4 quarts of water and bring to a boil. Reduce the heat to low and simmer for 1 hour.

3. Strain the broth through a fine-mesh strainer. Return the strained broth to the pot and bring to a gentle boil. Add the chopped celery and carrots, salt, turmeric, thyme, pepper, and the cayenne pepper (if using). Reduce the heat to medium-low and simmer for 10 minutes.

4. Add the egg noodles or orzo and cook 8 to 10 minutes, or until the noodles are tender.

5. Stir in the chicken. Taste and adjust the seasoning if necessary
    (I usually add another teaspoon of salt). Remove from the heat
    and let sit for 10 minutes before serving. Keeps for several days,
    refrigerated in a sealed container.

Meatloaf with Mashed-Potato Topping

Serves 6

For the Mashed-Potato Topping

6 medium potatoes, scrubbed, peeled, and cut into ½-inch chunks

1 teaspoon salt, divided

2 cups whole milk or half-and-half

½ stick (4 tablespoons) unsalted butter

¼ teaspoon freshly ground black pepper

For the Meatloaf

2 tablespoons olive oil

1 medium onion, finely chopped

1 green pepper, finely chopped

2 stalks celery, finely chopped

4 cloves garlic, finely chopped

1½ teaspoons salt, divided

½ teaspoon freshly ground black pepper

½ teaspoon dried thyme

½ teaspoon dried basil

2 pounds ground beef (ground chuck works well)

2 large eggs

½ cup half-and-half

¼ cup ketchup

2 teaspoons Worcestershire sauce

1½ teaspoons Dijon mustard

1 teaspoon ground paprika (whatever is your favorite kind)

⅔ cup dried breadcrumbs

To Make the Mashed-Potato Topping

1. Fill a large pot ¾ full with water and bring to a boil. Add the potatoes and ½ teaspoon of the salt and boil for approximately 15 minutes, until the potatoes are tender all the way through.

2. Strain the potatoes, then return them to the pot. Add the milk, butter, pepper, and the remaining ½ teaspoon of salt. Using a potato masher or wooden spoon, mash the potatoes to desired consistency. Taste and add more butter, milk, salt, or pepper as needed. Set aside and begin to prepare the meatloaf.

To Make the Meatloaf

1. Preheat the oven to 350°F.

2. In a large skillet over medium heat, warm the oil. Add the onion, green pepper, and celery and cook for 8 to 10 minutes, stirring occasionally. Add the garlic and cook for 1 additional minute, stirring.

3. Add ½ teaspoon of the salt as well as the pepper, thyme, and basil. Stir well to combine. Remove from the heat and set aside.

4. In a large bowl, crumble the ground beef. Set aside.

5. In a separate, medium bowl, whisk together the eggs. Add the half-and-half, ketchup, Worcestershire sauce, mustard, paprika, and remaining 1 teaspoon of the salt. Whisk together well. Set aside.

6. Take off any rings you're wearing and set them in a safe place.

7. Add the cooked vegetables to ground beef and stir to combine. Add the half-and-half mixture and the breadcrumbs and stir well. Get your hands in there to make sure it's very well blended.

8. Spoon the mixture into a 9 × 5-inch loaf pan and smooth the top. Bake for 45 minutes, then carefully remove from the oven, spread the mashed potatoes on top, and return to oven for 30 more minutes. The mashed potatoes should brown a bit on top—you can broil for 1 minute or so if necessary.

9. Let the meatloaf rest for 10 or so minutes before slicing and serving.

New York Strip

For special occasions.

Serves 2–3 hungry cave people

2 8–10-ounce New York strip steaks, 1¼–1½ inches thick

Salt, for rubbing

Freshly ground black pepper, for rubbing

Olive oil, for rubbing

1. Sprinkle both each side of the steaks with 1 pinch of salt and pepper. Set aside.

2. Heat a griddle, grill pan, or skillet (cast iron is best) over high heat, 3 to 4 minutes, until very hot—the surface should be smoking a little.

3. Rub olive oil on both sides of the steak, then cook for 5 to 7 minutes on each side, 3 to 4 minutes for medium-rare or 5 to 6 minutes for medium. Remove from the heat and let sit for 2 to 3 minutes before serving.

CHAPTER THREE

Mostly Plants

JONAH WAS LOOKING THIN AND STRETCHED OUT. "I think I am losing weight," he said, in response to my concern. Yep, it was official: I was the world's worst mother. I asked him what he'd been eating for lunch, usually his biggest meal of the day, the meal that really had to sustain him that autumn through the long afternoons of his senior year.

"Umm, salad," he said. "An apple."

My son was eating like an anorexic girl.

It might as well have been a foreign country, or another planet, as strange and dazzling as it was. It was only Duxbury, Massachusetts, an elegant seaside New England town, but it seemed to me like the exact opposite of my southern Indiana home. And there I was, in the summer of 1986, sprawled on the family room rug of my new friend Juliana, doing what we'd been doing together since we'd met a few months earlier: listening to records and talking about music.

I don't miss much about my youth, which I have vicariously relived as my kids have sprung into teenagers and young adults. I wouldn't go back to all the chaos, drama, and insecurity. I am happier in my forties than I've ever been. But the one thing I do miss, achingly, is listening to music with friends for hours on end, albums spread out across the floor, the drop of the needle, the possibility that everything might be just about to change. For me, in that Duxbury family room, everything was indeed about to change.

I'd met Juliana Hatfield that spring at Boston's Berklee College of Music, where she was a student, as was my boyfriend John. The three of us had been eyeballing each other for months, and when we finally met, we connected instantly. We agreed to start a band—the Blake Babies—the very night we met. That night we sat in Juliana's dorm room and she played us a song she'd written. I instantly loved her tough, girlish voice. But right after we'd established this exciting new venture, John headed home to Indiana for the summer, leaving Juliana and me to kick around Boston on our own. Juliana wasn't like anybody I'd ever met, and she was very different from me—shy, quiet, intensely opinionated, and fiercely disciplined. She didn't drink or smoke, she practiced guitar zealously, and she was more than happy to spend hours alone working on her songs. Two things we had in common, though, were that we loved music and we were very, very happy to have found each other. We played together as best we could, setting up in the crappy studio apartment that I shared with two other people and cobbled together an amp or two, a microphone, and an old drum set. We worked on Juliana's fledgling songs and bashed through some covers, mostly Replacements songs. At other times, we hung out in the much more comfortable apartment that she shared with a few Boston University students. We usually listened to records there, to the bands that Juliana loved intensely—like X, her biggest obsession. In between, we walked the streets of Boston, her in jeans, white T-shirts, and enormous black oxfords, with poker-straight, dark-brown hair and arrestingly bright blue eyes, and me in cotton print dresses and combat boots, wearing a messy blonde ponytail and a big smile. We were eighteen. "Hey," Juliana whispered, as we walked down Newbury Street one evening, "I think people are looking at us." "God, why?" I said stupidly, to the prettiest girl I'd ever known. "What's *wrong* with us?"

That summer is mostly a hazy blur to me now, as happy as it was intense and challenging. I'd been playing for a year or so, and I loved the way drumming felt, but it was still a physical struggle. The instrument often seemed to get the better of me, overwhelmed me. I was grappling with the whole concept of starting a band and trying to become a professional musician. I wasn't ready as a player, and I knew it, but I wanted it badly enough. Maybe that would see me through. I was also working as a full-time office assistant at Harvard. It was a real, grown-up job that I had faked my way into and, at bottom, wasn't really qualified to hold. Everybody else my age was in college, working a part-time job, still mostly supported by their parents, and I was pretending to be an adult, with a job and a band and an apartment. My family, home, and childhood felt far away. No wonder I leapt at Juliana's invitation to spend the weekend in Duxbury. I was ready to see our friendship deepen, but I was also ready to be in a calm, safe place. I anticipated parents, siblings, clean sheets, food in the refrigerator. Normal things.

Juliana and I made our way to Duxbury through a haphazard combination of bus travel, hitchhiking, and stumbling blind along the pitch-black shoulder of a Massachusetts road. We made it to her family's big, elegant old house, where her glamorous mom, sharp stepdad, and cute blond brothers casually welcomed Juliana's ragamuffiny drummer friend into the family fold. It was lovely. We had the run of the place and did what we wanted, shambling all weekend back and forth between the beach and the house, from the fridge to the television to the stereo in the family room. The records we listened to that weekend were the ones Juliana didn't love enough to bring with her to Boston, bands she had been into in high school. Like The Smiths.

I'd managed to miss out entirely on The Smiths, a seminal band for many of my generation, so I asked her to play me a few songs. I liked them OK. The music was soaring and emotional in a way that I could appreciate, but the songs didn't make my heart pound like X, the Replacements, or Hüsker Dü. Then she dropped the needle on "Meat is Murder." And I was riveted. "Play that one again," I said, and I listened hard, reading the lyric sheet (another great and sorely missed aspect of the album listening ritual).

"And death for no reason is murder," sang Morrissey. This strident claim bypassed the questioning part of my brain, went straight to my heart, and I was converted, instantly. Perhaps it was just a matter of the right conditions being in place—had I been thinking already about becoming vegetarian? Maybe Morrissey was *right*; I still wonder about this, although my views on vegetarianism are unclear and complicated these days. Maybe it's just that I was eighteen and impressionable. Or maybe there was something about being in Duxbury with Juliana that made me want to change, that made me want to not be my old self anymore but something new and different and better.

I can't say I'm not embarrassed by this admission—not embarrassed that I became vegetarian but that it was a Smiths song that made me do it. It is pretty telling that I've never confessed the details of my conversion before now. But it was a pivotal moment and yet another instance in which music and food intertwined, as a singer and his song affected every bite I would take for the rest of my life. Furthermore, I shared the experience with a kindred spirit, my new band mate. By November of that year, the Blake Babies would play our first gig, in a Boston used clothing store. Juliana and I would go on to work together, off and on, for twenty years, making seven records in two different bands. Records that girls might spread out on family room floors, onto which needles might drop, and to which, hopefully, a few hearts might pound. And there would be tours together around the US, where we would scan menus and search for vegetarian options and settle, too often, on something that really wasn't enough. We'd get too skinny, especially Juliana, but I took some nourishment from the sense of rightness I felt from making a conscious decision about something I did everyday.

It had been two weeks since seventeen-year-old Jonah had announced his intention to be vegan for a month. I'd begun to expect the unexpected from my late-blooming teen, and I had welcomed the plants-only experiment. But I should have been giving him more support. I had learned the hard way that this diet can pose nutritional challenges, and not just for touring musicians. During one strictly vegan phase in my life, I'd lost fifteen non-extra pounds and stopped menstruating. Eventually, I figured out how to get enough protein, fat, and calories to be a perfectly healthy vegan (it is definitely possible!), but it didn't come automatically. Now I was abandoning Jonah to his own clueless devices and my thin son was getting thinner.

"Hummus," I said. "I am going to teach you how to make hummus." I'd been meaning to offer that lesson for a while, but the fall was crazy with the boys back in school, Jake teaching a heavy load at Northwestern, and my administrative job in full swing. It had become all too easy to blow off our cooking lessons. But it was hummus time, and hummus came to the rescue, the first of many times that month that beans would save the day. Hummus is the the vegan's high-protein, nutrient-dense best friend. Jonah started packing his lunch with my help—two huge hummus sandwiches loaded with sprouts and lettuce, a big bag of carrot sticks, an apple, and a thermos of green tea. That was more like it. When he got bored, I taught him some other sandwich options—a luscious cashew and red pepper "cheese" and a savory tempeh mock-chicken salad. His weight bounced right back to normal. Once he started doing it right, the vegan diet agreed with Jonah.

In fact, Jonah's motivation for this dietary experiment was cosmetic. He was about the same age I'd been when I had my come-to-Morrissey moment in Duxbury, but he hadn't stopped eating animals for ethical or emotional reasons. He got the idea from his dermatologist. Like most teenagers, Jonah had acne, and he was getting fed up. I could relate. I've always been prone to breakouts, and even as an adult I can't get away with overindulging in greasy food or booze. When I was a teenager, my doctor insisted that there was no connection between diet and acne, but Jonah's doctor told him otherwise and shared convincing research that linked beef and dairy consumption with skin inflammation. Jonah had enough discipline to give it a try. I was glad that he was thinking about food in a more conscious and complicated way and that he was learning how to cook and take care of himself. His experiment fed fortuitously into my plans to bring food and cooking to the forefront of our family conversations and more concretely into Jonah's day-to-day reality.

From vegan sandwich spreads we moved on to Beans 101. Here was another way Jonah's vegan experiment was fortuitous—this was a good month for eating lots of beans. We were recovering from the expense of moving, as well as from the salary decrease that accompanied my new job, and beans are easy on the budget. Overall, I have a tendency to spend too much on food. Granted, Americans as a whole are too willing to buy a lot of cheap, poor-quality food, but our family was living paycheck to paycheck, and I really knew better than to be so seduced by Whole Foods—its pricey bakery, fancy deli, and enticing shelves of convenience food. Whenever I start to feel nauseous at check-out, when the teller announces the total and it's way too much, I resolve *we must eat more beans!*

That month, we certainly did. I taught Jonah how to make a simple white bean soup and a mixed-bean chili. The latter got us through three dinners in various iterations (plain chili; huevos rancheros; mixed bean tacos). I did some math and told Jonah how much a big bowl of our delicious chili cost: less than a dollar! And we were using canned beans; it would have been even cheaper had we used dried. "Wow," said Jonah. "I guess I'll live off of beans in college." Exactly.

Jonah and I met in the kitchen to make baked beans, another simple classic. I was trying to identify his style in the kitchen, his approach to cooking. I'm a messy cook, a slightly wild one, not a clean-up-as-I-go-along one. But I am definitely a recipe person. I don't always follow them to a T, but I almost always refer to one when I cook. I know some cooks scoff at recipes; some are too at-tention-deficit to follow them, some don't trust them, and I guess the real geniuses don't need them at all. But what about Jonah? Would he be into making it up as he went along, or would he be a recipe follower like me?

For the cooking lesson, we followed my baked bean recipe, one I've developed over time but that still never seemed quite perfect. I encouraged Jonah to taste often and adjust the seasoning and al-lowed him to make all the decisions. He liked this; he added more cayenne, more mustard, less molasses. It was a fun, easy lesson and it set the mood to tackle a difficult subject. So while we tin-kered with bottles of maple syrup and ketchup and jars of ginger and cayenne, and spooned little bite-fulls into our mouths, I asked him about college applications. I'd been avoiding the subject but had been obsessing about it to myself ever since the fall semester had started. "Isn't it time," I said, trying to be light and casual, "to do some research? Make a plan?" Jonah's face darkened. So did the mood. "I will," he said. "Don't worry about it."

I was worried. One of the undergraduate work-study students that I supervised at Northwestern had told me about her senior year of high school and the system of organization she'd set up to keep track of her college search. She'd had a binder. Jonah did *not* have a binder.

"Really," I said, "it's time to make a plan for this stuff." He stirred the beans, took one last taste, and finally approved the seasoning. We put them in the oven to bake while I whipped up a batch of cornbread and Jonah prepared a pot of steamed kale. He refused to respond to my college nagging, and eventually I gave up and we finished cooking dinner in silence. Yeah, maybe Jonah wasn't going to be a recipe guy. Maybe he was a make-it-up-as-you-go-along guy. In the case of our baked beans, it worked out fine. They were very tasty. As far as the next chapter in his life went, that remained to be seen.

It wasn't a big stretch for me to see cooking as a metaphor for all the life skills I was not effectively transmitting to my sons—skills related to preparation, planning, and independence, everything I was somehow trying to squeeze into that year of cooking lessons. For my kids, food just seemed to land on the table every night at the same time. There was always enough of it, it was always edible, sometimes it was really good, and it was always there, something they could take for granted.

When I was a kid, it wasn't always this way, and in some ways I benefitted from that. I grew up with a single mother who worked full time, editing a university magazine, and who still managed to put dinner on the table nearly every night. We ate good dinners: spaghetti with homemade tomato sauce; big, fresh salads; beef stroganoff with thick egg noodles; corned beef hash with soft boiled eggs. But there were some nights when she worked late and my brother and I had to fend for ourselves. I was the oldest, so it fell on me to make dinner. I have a distinct memory of being ten years old and carefully following the recipe in *The Joy of Cooking* for scrambled eggs down to the exact tablespoonful of cream (a recipe follower from the start). When the eggs turned out as good as any I'd ever eaten, I had an epiphany: Cooking was not some big mystery, but rather simply a matter of following instructions and having the right ingredients on hand. I was hooked. I spent hours poring over *The Joy of Cooking*, and even though many of the recipes were complicated and out of reach, I marveled over the beauty of the simple and more accessible ones.

I attribute a certain amount of my love of cooking to that classic cookbook, but I owe just as much to those strange, lonely evenings at home without a parent, scrounging up something to eat. The whole '70s-style parent thing came with some fringe benefits, and although I'm glad my children have had a more stable childhood than I did, I also wish I'd found more ways to help them learn to take care of themselves. I consider it a failing that they just sit down at the table and expect food to land in front of them. They have no idea how much time Jake and I spend planning meals, making lists, buying groceries, preparing food. Even as I sit and write, far from the domestic scene, I have it in the back of my mind that I want to cook a pot of brown rice tonight so that when I get home tired and hungry from work tomorrow, I can chop up some vegetables and make a quick fried rice. How could I acclimate Jonah to this kind of planning?

Beans, again, to the rescue. I decided to give him a lesson in making a pot of refried beans from scratch, starting the day before by soaking the beans overnight. It's not hard work, but requires some forethought. For our other bean recipes, we'd relied on canned beans, which were fine, but I wanted him to see the whole process of preparation from beginning to end. He seemed a little disoriented when I called him out of his room at night to wash and soak a pound of pinto beans in cold water for the following night's burrito supper.

The next evening I showed him how to drain, rinse, and cook the pintos. They take just over an hour to cook, so during that time we chopped and grated our burrito toppings, warmed the tortillas, and set the table. When the beans were finished we set everything out on the table in bowls for a make-your-own-burrito bar. We tore into everything ravenously and devoured our burritos in minutes. Jonah watched as Jake piled a tortilla high for a second serving. "Hey," he said. "How about some thanks?" He paused. "I've been working on these since *last night*."

The Beans 101 intensive course was winding down, and we had another lapse between cooking lessons. Jonah was on the run, hanging out with friends, starting driving lessons, keeping up with a heavy homework load, and enjoying the last mild days of the year. He seemed to be hanging out exclusively with his guy friends and didn't mention his girlfriend anymore, so I assumed they'd broken up. I could never get him in a room long enough to ask. I finally managed to lasso him for a quick lesson on mujadarrah, a simple lentil and rice dish, but it wasn't exactly quality time together; as we cooked, he texted with his friends, and the moment we were finished he shot out the door. I was making the dish as a contribution to a potluck with our new neighbors, the first such group gathering since we'd moved in a month earlier. Our upstairs neighbors had come around earlier that day and suggested the potluck after scoring a mother lode of the season's last tomatoes from the Evanston farmers market. I happened to be making an outrageous chocolate cake that afternoon, along with the more monkish lentils and rice, and I was delighted by the invitation. Floor three said yes too, and so we had a plan.

After Jonah's hasty departure, I assumed he wouldn't join us, but just in case, Jake sent him a quick text as dinnertime grew near: *Are you sure you don't want to come to this potluck?* He stunned me by turning up a few minutes later. The promise of all that food was too much to resist. So our family of four joined second-floor neighbors Francesca and Laura and third-floor resident and landlady Mary Ellen in the well-tended garden behind our building. It was the last warm evening of the year, and we sat out for hours, lighting candles when it got too dark to see, lingering over wine and food, huddling around the two rickety little tables we'd pushed together. I thought again about the function of the dinner table and how it was important to extend it beyond the nuclear family sometimes. This was something we hadn't done much since our big move across the ocean. It was good to be reminded of this basic way to connect and feel a sense of community. And I love potlucks. Francesca and Laura had transformed their tomatoes into a fresh sauce with basil, tossed with pasta; Mary Ellen brought a kale and goat cheese tart, light and savory, and the lentils and rice dish, with caramelized onions, were a heavenly match with the fresh tomatoes. It was a fairly virtuous dinner, and we were rewarded for it with my decadent chocolate cake.

Jonah stayed on and on. He was downright charming with the neighbors, friendly and chatty while talking about high school and the prospect of college. College! I'd still not managed to have a productive conversation with him on the subject after several dismal attempts, and now, seemingly from nowhere, names of colleges dropped from his lips as if he talked about it all the time. Here was another argument for the presence of a community beyond the immediate family.

"Northern Arizona," I heard him say, "Oregon. Colorado." I listened with my mouth open while he explained to our neighbors that he was drawn to the American West. *Who are you*, I thought. It was disorienting, but also kind of hilarious, and it drove home the fact that he was his own person, with a lot more going on inside than could be squeezed out by force. Our experiences were different, but in some fundamental ways he was a lot like I'd been, stumbling down a dark Massachusetts highway, trusting I'd reach my destination, or sitting on my friend's family room floor, unconsciously setting a course for my life.

I kept sneaking peeks at him that evening, watching while he happily ate and chatted. He looked great. His skin was clearer, and his eyes were too, without that worrying bleariness of the summer. He smiled often and looked right at people when he spoke to them. He complimented everybody's food enthusiastically. OK, my son didn't have a college binder. But maybe I didn't need to worry about him so much. Or maybe I could at least take a little break from worrying every now and then.

After Jonah left to meet his friends again ("Wow," he said, before he left, "I didn't think I'd stay here this long,") and Henry went inside for bed, our neighbors, who were starting to feel a little like friends, praised the boys: "Your kids are great. Delightful." I let myself bask in that while we basked in the candlelight of autumn's last hurrah.

The vegan month was ending. Where would we go from here? Certainly not back to meat and potatoes. Had Jonah had a conversion experience of his own?

"Nah," he said.

I keep looping back to how similar Jonah and I are, while at the same time banging hard up against our differences. I stopped eating meat out of passion, and that decision still, in part, defines me. He stopped eating meat as an experiment, to clear up his skin a bit. I cooked dinner as a kid because I had to. He cooks now because I suggest that he do so, because I am teaching him.

"But" said Jonah, "I think I will keep avoiding dairy, and not eat as much meat as I ate before." In other words, pretty much back to normal for our family, our ordinary mostly-veggie mish-mash. Sometimes I envy families with a more definitive stance on diet, whether the cheerful meat eaters with shopping carts full of lamb chops or the careful vegans studying the ingredients on every loaf of bread. I've never quite been one of them. I've called myself vegetarian, off and on, for most of my life now, and I like the definition and clarity it has lent my identity, the focus it has given to my food choices and, again, that sense of consciousness and rightness. My initial inspiration for giving up meat was musical, emotional, and impulsive, but over the years I've acquired more substantive knowledge to bolster that decision. I read Frances Moore Lappe's *Diet for a Small Planet* and took to heart her arguments about world hunger and the resource-draining practices of the meat industry. I read about T. Colin Campbell's *The China Study*, which provided statistical links between the consumption of meat, dairy, and eggs to the diseases that kill most of us—heart disease, cancer, diabetes. I watched John Robbins's documentary, *Diet for a New America*, and was deeply disturbed by its depictions of crowded, unsanitary factory farms. And yet I have landed here as "mostly vegetarian" for reasons I don't often consider.

For one thing, it's a chore to resist the cultural and social prevalence of animal food. Eating fish, something I've often allowed myself, makes ordering in restaurants or going to dinner parties easier. During those stretches in my life when I've been strictly vegetarian or vegan I've felt like a rebel, a renegade, which I enjoy. It can be a fun and satisfying identity to embrace, but it can get tiresome: One can long to rejoin the happy pizza-eating masses. And to further complicate matters, that part of me that enjoys the rebellion of veganism also rebels against the strict rules of veganism.

At any rate, I have strayed from my most strident idealism, but this vegan month rekindled some of these thoughts about the multivalent benefits of avoiding, or at least minimizing, animal food. It is, truly, a lighter way to live on the planet. I can take solace in the fact that others who think a great deal about these matters are also looking for a middle path—consider Michael Pollan's injunction that we should eat "mostly plants" or Mark Bittman's interesting proposal that we try being "vegan before six." I think I'm not the only one who has struggled to live strictly in any particular camp. And I guess it's no surprise that my kids follow suit.

Maybe the wishy-washiness that bugs me in myself has been more instructive than I realized. I could see that my sons had some room to think about food and to play around with how and what they want to eat (and maybe where and why they want to go to college). I'd been focusing on the technical aspects of teaching Jonah how to cook, but of course food is much more than cooking techniques, just as it's much more than simple sustenance. What we eat can define us to ourselves and can communicate our identities, in all their permutations, to others. This has certainly been the case for me. From young vegetarian rocker to middle-aged flexitarian mom, I always answered my own internal questions about who I am in terms of food. Maybe I was indirectly teaching my children to be flexible, to adapt. But above all, I hoped, I was teaching them to be conscious, to be aware of the incredible range of choices we face with every bite of food we consume, and the meanings and implications in those choices. The vegan month was ending, but I could hear its reverberations echoing on.

Spicy Hummus

Serves 6

Zest of 1 lemon

½ teaspoon salt

2 garlic cloves

2 15-ounce cans chickpeas, drained

3 tablespoons tahini

2 tablespoons fresh lemon juice

1½ teaspoons ground cumin

¼ teaspoon ground cayenne pepper

2 tablespoons olive oil, plus more for drizzling

Ground hot paprika, for garnish

Minced fresh parsley, for garnish

1. In a food processor, pulse together the lemon zest and salt. Add the garlic and pulse another 10 times or so. Add the chickpeas, tahini, lemon juice, cumin, and cayenne pepper, as well as 5 tablespoons of water, and process for 1 to 2 minutes, until well combined.

2. With the food processor running, add the olive oil in a steady stream and process for 3 to 4 minutes, until the hummus is very smooth and creamy. If necessary, add additional water, ½ tablespoon at a time, to get the consistency you want. For the best flavor, refrigerate the hummus for at least 1 hour before serving.

3. Serve garnished with olive oil, paprika, and parsley.

Red Pepper–Cashew Spread

Adapted from a recipe in *May All Be Fed*, by John Robbins. A vegan treat, and a more-than-suitable substitute for cream cheese. Amazing on a toasted bagel or in a wrap with lettuce, tomato, and sprouts. Keeps for 3 or 4 days in the fridge.

Serves 6

4 tablespoons olive oil

1 small red bell pepper, seeded and chopped

1½ cups cashews

¼ cup hemp or sesame seeds

¼ cup nutritional yeast flakes

¼ cup fresh lemon juice

1 tablespoon soy sauce

1. In a small pan or skillet over medium heat, warm the olive oil. Add the bell pepper and cook for 7 or 8 minutes, or until tender.

2. Transfer the pepper and oil to a blender or food processor, add the remaining ingredients as well as ¼ cup of water, and blend until smooth and creamy.

3. For best flavor, refrigerate for at least 1 hour before serving.

Tempeh Mock-Chicken Salad

This is an old-school health-food recipe that I used to make every week when I was strictly vegan. Good on crackers or sandwiches. For a delicious lunch, double the recipe (except tempeh) and combine with 2 cups of cooked pasta (corn macaroni works well).

Serves 4

2 teaspoons tamari soy sauce, divided

1 teaspoon mirin (sweet rice wine)

8 ounces tempeh, cubed into ½-inch pieces

4 tablespoons eggless mayonnaise

2 heaping tablespoons chopped dill pickles

2 tablespoons nutritional yeast

2 tablespoons minced fresh parsley

1 tablespoon dijon mustard

1 stalk celery, finely chopped

1. In a medium bowl, whisk 1 teaspoon of the tamari together with the mirin and 1 tablespoon of water. Marinate the tempeh in this mixture for 10 minutes. The tempeh will absorb the marinade.

2. In a medium pot fitted with a steamer over medium heat, steam the tempeh for 15 minutes. Set aside to cool completely.

3. In a medium bowl, combine the rest of the ingredients, including the remaining teaspoon of tamari, and mix well. Add the tempeh, taste, and adjust seasoning as needed. Refrigerate for at least 1 hour before serving.

Spinach and White Bean Stew

This stew is deeply flavorful, as if you worked on it for hours, but it comes together in just 15 minutes thanks to the canned beans and pre-washed baby spinach. This was a great recipe to teach to my teenage son—it's foolproof! One of my favorite winter lunches or quick suppers, best served with a baguette or hunk of good bread.

Serves 3–4

4 tablespoons olive oil, plus more for drizzling, optional

4 cloves garlic, thinly sliced

3 15-ounce cans small white beans, drained

1 scant tablespoon dried thyme

1½-pound bag pre-washed baby spinach or baby kale

½ teaspoon salt

½ teaspoon red pepper flakes, plus more for sprinkling, optional

¼ teaspoon freshly ground black pepper

1. In a large pot over medium heat, warm the olive oil. Add the garlic and cook for 1 minute, stirring constantly. Add the beans, thyme, and 2 cups of water, and bring to a gentle boil. Reduce the heat to medium-low and simmer, uncovered, for 10 minutes.

2. Add the spinach or kale in big handfuls, stirring to incorporate. Add the salt, red pepper flakes, and pepper. Taste and adjust seasoning as needed. Remove from the heat and let cool for a few minutes to allow the flavors to meld. Drizzle with additional olive oil and top with additional red pepper flakes on top, if desired. Serve warm.

Vegetarian Baked Beans

Serves 6

4 tablespoons olive oil, divided

1 medium onion, finely chopped

1 teaspoon sea salt, plus more for cooking the onion

4 15-ounce cans navy beans, liquid reserved

½ cup ketchup

¼ cup molasses

3 tablespoons shoyu or tamari, or any soy sauce

2 tablespoons maple syrup

1 tablespoon mustard powder

¼ teaspoon ground cayenne pepper

1 6-ounce package smoky tempeh strips, chopped into ½-inch pieces

1. Preheat the oven to 325°F.

2. In a large ovenproof pot over medium heat, warm 2 tablespoons of the olive oil. Add the onion and a small pinch of salt and cook 15 minutes, stirring occasionally, until the onion is tender and sweet but not brown.

3. Add all of the ingredients from the beans through the cayenne pepper. Stir and bring to a gentle simmer. Taste and adjust seasoning as needed. Cover and transfer to the oven. Bake 1½-2 hours, stirring every 30 minutes, until the liquid is mostly absorbed and the beans are saucy.

4. While the beans are baking, warm the remaining 2 tablespoons of oil in a skillet and add the tempeh. Cook, stirring frequently, for 5 to 10 minutes to brown. Stir the tempeh into bean pot after about an hour. Serve warm.

Vegetarian Refried Bean Burritos

Adapted from a recipe in *Fresh From a Vegetarian Kitchen*, by Meredith McCarthy

Makes 4–6 burritos

1 pound (2½ cups) dried pinto beans

1 6-inch piece kombu sea vegetable, optional

1 fresh bay leaf

3 tablespoons olive oil

2 tablespoons soy sauce

1 teaspoon sea salt, plus more to taste

Big pinch ground cayenne pepper, optional

4–6 flour or corn tortillas

Toppings, to taste: lettuce, tomato, avocado, salsa, whatever you like

1. Rinse and drain the beans. Soak in 6 cups of cold water for at least 8 hours. Drain the beans.

2. In a large pot, combine the beans with 6 cups of fresh water, the kombu, and the bay leaf. Bring to a boil, cover, reduce the heat to medium and simmer the beans 1½ to 2 hours, until very tender. Add more water if necessary to keep the beans just covered.

3. In a large skillet over medium heat, warm the oil. Add the beans and enough of the beans' cooking water to cover (I usually end up using all the cooking water). Remove and discard the bay leaf and kombu bits if you want (they may have dissolved, that's perfectly fine). Add the soy sauce and salt. Stir and mash the beans until they become thick and saucy, about 15 minutes. Taste and add more salt if necessary, and cayenne pepper if desired.

4. Heat a medium skillet over medium heat, then one at a time, add the tortillas and warm about 15 seconds on each side. Stack on a plate and set aside.

5. Transfer the beans to a large bowl and set up a make-your-own-burrito bar with toppings in individual bowls. Then watch all your hard work disappear. Leftover refried beans will keep for a couple of days in the refrigerator, and make a tasty dip for corn chips.

NOTE: Kombu makes the beans tender, tasty, and digestible, and adds healthy minerals. Adding kombu is my number-one tip when cooking beans, one of the few I've hung onto from my macrobiotic days. It's worth buying a bag at the health-food store or Japanese grocery. Also, fun fact: MSG was concocted in the early twentieth century as an attempt to emulate the flavor-enhancing glutamates in seaweeds like kombu.

Lentils and Caramelized Onions with Capellini

A riff on mujadarrah, with pasta instead of rice and red pepper instead of cumin. I think this dish is way more than the sum of its parts; it's really rich and satisfying for so few and such simple ingredients. One tester, who cooked this for himself and his wife, wrote, "I liked the dish, but *she* thought it was like Jesus returning and breaking the cross over his knee."

Serves 4

6 tablespoons olive oil

2 medium yellow onions, very thinly sliced

¾ teaspoon salt, plus more for cooking onions and pasta

¾ cup dried green lentils, rinsed and drained

8 ounces capellini pasta

¼ teaspoon freshly ground black pepper

Red pepper flakes, for garnish

1 small handful fresh parsley, finely chopped, for garnish

1. In a large, deep skillet, warm the oil over high heat. Add the onions and cook, stirring constantly, until they start to sizzle. Add a generous pinch of salt, stir well, and reduce heat to medium-low. Cover and cook for 5 minutes undisturbed. Uncover and cook 15 or so more minutes, stirring occasionally, until the onions are sweet and delicious and you are tempted to eat them on the spot with a spoon. Resist.

2. While the onions are caramelizing, bring a large pot ¾ full with water to a boil over high heat. Add the lentils, reduce the heat to medium, and simmer for 20 minutes, or until the lentils are tender but intact. Some lentils are tougher than others—you'll want to taste to make sure they're right; al dente is what you're going for. Keep the water level constant, adding more if necessary as the water evaporates and gets absorbed by the lentils, because you are going to add pasta to the mix soon.

3. After the lentils have cooked 20 minutes, add the capellini along with a generous pinch of salt and cook 3 to 4 minutes, or according to package directions, until the pasta is al dente. Drain and return to the pot. Gently stir in the caramelized onions, ¾ teaspoon of salt, and the pepper. Taste and adjust seasoning as needed.

4. Serve warm, garnished with lots of red pepper flakes and chopped parsley.

CHAPTER FOUR

Wok and Roll

"**T**HIS RICE IS BLAND," said Jonah. He did not often complain about my cooking.

"It's *rice*. It tastes like *rice*. What is it *supposed* to taste like?" I said.

"I don't know," said Jonah, "but Jacob's dad's rice has *flavor*."

This had been happening all week, since Jonah's return from an autumn visit with his childhood friend Jacob in our old hometown of Bloomington, Indiana. Nothing I cooked measured up to the high standard set by Jacob's dad. Not my scrambled eggs, until then undisputedly the best in the world; not my roasted vegetables, always a hit in the past; and apparently not my rice. I made a mental note to find out what was going on with that rice, and tried to tone down my irritation. I honestly had no right to be irritated. If you believe in karma, I'd had this coming to me for thirty years.

"This isn't spicy at all," I said to my mother, when I was sixteen, over a perfectly good plate of spaghetti and meatballs at home. "John's dad makes spicy noodles with fresh chili peppers." "Oh," said my mom. "Well." She bristled, but bit her tongue. Perhaps she was growing accustomed to such blunt adolescent comparisons.

John was John Strohm, my high school boyfriend. In a couple of years we would leave Bloomington for Boston, and together we would knock on Juliana Hatfield's dorm room door to ask if she wanted to start a band with us. But back then we were surviving high school and falling in love. John was already an active musician, drumming in Midwestern punk bands with names that made our parents laugh or roll their eyes, like Killing Children or Yellow Rain. The Indiana punk scene was blossoming into a small but mighty force, with bands like the Zero Boys and the Gizmos at the forefront and dozens of others forming a ragtag community and releasing records on small independent labels. These bands created a circuit for live performances outside the mainstream venues. Gigs might be in thrift stores, old schools, the basements of coffee shops, or out on the streets of Bloomington, where the local cable radio station, WQAX, sponsored legendary street dances on summer nights. I was already listening to a handful of '70s punk records when I met John—I loved the Clash and the Sex Pistols—but dating an active musician plunged me into the live punk scene. It was a good place to be. I connected with the spirit of nonconformity and the do-it-yourself ethic. It all felt fresh and exciting and in contrast to my high school world, where I wasn't inspired by many of my classes and couldn't relate to the culture of jocks and cheerleaders.

John and I thought of ourselves as punks, although there were definitely punker punks around—kids with Mohawks, chains, and piercings. John was the coolest looking guy I'd ever seen; he was tall and skinny, with a charmingly crooked face and a low-key David Bowie-esque mullet. He wore striped button-up shirts that he bought in thrift stores, or tee shirts emblazoned with the names of hardcore punk bands. I had my own David Bowie-esque mullet (that was, briefly, dyed purple) and wore vintage dresses and miniskirts. But to us being punk mostly meant that we went to shows, shopped in record stores downtown—not in the sterile suburban mall—and relished being outsiders in our mostly conservative surroundings. In the early days of my romance with John, I went with him to the shows where he performed, helped him carry his drums, learned how to set them up, and then watched from the sidelines while he played.

The exact moment I mastered the art of carrying, setting up, and breaking down a drum set was the exact moment I grew weary of being a band girlfriend. I wanted in on the fun.

There was nothing in my world at the time that suggested it was notable or even interesting that a girl wanted to play drums. It's true that there weren't many girls doing it, a fact that confounded me then and that confounds and frustrates me even today, but I didn't think about the decision as a statement, an act of rebellion, or any kind of radical step. I was raised by a feminist mom who signed me up for all-boy softball and hockey leagues even though I was skinny and unathletic; I was part of an open-minded community of music-loving punks; and I had a really, really cool boyfriend. Down in the basement of his divorced father's handsome limestone bungalow, when my work was done at The Daily Bread, John showed me how to play a basic drumbeat. Then he picked up the guitar that he'd been learning how to play, we broke into "Sweet Jane," and boom I was a drummer.

John's dad, Paul Strohm, was tolerant of our noisy jams in his basement. In fact, as cool as my boyfriend was, his dad was maybe even cooler. Paul Strohm was an English professor, wrote and published short stories, went on Zen meditation retreats, was an accomplished and inventive cook, and was the only parent I'd ever met who really followed current music and bought new records. I appreciated and still appreciate the excellent music I grew up with—the Beatles, the Rolling Stones, and Bob Dylan—but Paul Strohm had all these plus records by Talking Heads, Leonard Cohen, and Dire Straits. The Strohms were close friends with music writer Anthony DeCurtis, who would eventually become an editor at *Rolling Stone*, and a fresh supply of music sprang from Anthony's passionate recommendations.

One of these recommendations was for a new band from Athens, Georgia, that Anthony happened to see live and write about a few times, right on the brink of their first release. R.E.M. didn't sound anything like *anything* on the radio, and though this band didn't sound much like the punk bands we were following, there was a clear kinship there. The sound startled me. Peter Buck seemed to be inventing a new way to play guitar, and Michael Stipe's mysterious mumbling reminded me of nothing I'd ever heard. "This is a new thing," I remember saying to John, "and I have a weird feeling we're going to be part of it."

"What is that?" I asked John, who was scraping the tan skin off a knobby root and mincing up its stringy flesh. "It's ginger," he said, looking embarrassed on my behalf. But Paul Strohm, working in the kitchen alongside John, didn't flinch. This was southern Indiana in 1983. Ginger root was not yet part of mainstream food culture. The thing is, I didn't consider myself to be part of mainstream food culture either. All my life I'd felt like a freak, food-wise. My mother refused to buy soda, unlike everyone else's mother I knew ("What do you even drink?" asked my friends). No white bread, no Captain Crunch, no Twinkies. When I was young, I'd dreamed of being an adult, able to eat whatever I wanted. Pop Tarts for lunch. I'd always complained about my all-natural peanut butter sandwiches on brown bread, but John complained about his tahini and honey sandwiches on pita bread. ("What's tahini?" I asked.) My dreams of a Pop-Tart diet were losing their allure the more time I spent in the Strohm household. Eating food that other people didn't eat—like listening to music that other people didn't listen to—appealed to my little punk soul. Food choices provided another way to be interesting and alternative.

John was preparing that ginger for a stir-fry, the first one I remember eating in my life, and I was engrossed in watching it all come together. The setting itself was mesmerizing. Paul Strohm had a serious cook's kitchen: a sturdy six-burner gas range, where a pot of rice bubbled away; an herb garden outside the kitchen window, from which he had harvested a handful of cilantro; a wooden chopping-block countertop piled with garlic, peppers, spinach, green onions; jars of spices and sauces, most of them new to me—fermented black bean sauce, chili garlic sauce, hot pepper oil. John and Paul peeled, chopped, and whisked.

"Chopping vegetables is relaxing," said Paul. He periodically spent time at the Green Gulch Farm Zen Center in California, where he would alternate sitting in meditation with working in the gardens or the kitchen, and he'd picked up a certain attitude toward domestic work that I'd never encountered before, a kind of calm focus. He pulled out a beat-up cast-iron pot, bowl-shaped and deep with a long handle. "This is my wok," he said. I'd never seen one of those, either. He heated it over a high flame, then flung a few drops of water in. "When they dance, it's ready," said Paul. He poured in a glug of peanut oil. "It can take very high heat without starting to smoke," he explained. In went the vegetables, hardest first, then softer. Then the sauce, then everything onto plates of hot rice. We sat down to enjoy this bright, hot, spicy treat, and I was hooked. Pop-Tarts? No thank you.

Just as I wasn't content to be a band girlfriend forever, I wasn't satisfied on the sidelines of the Strohm kitchen. I wanted in on the action. Two years after that memorable stir-fry, I'd find myself a key player in a major event: a pizza party to celebrate John's graduation from high school (I'd graduated a year earlier). I had some professional baking experience under my belt by then, which put me in charge of making the crusts. John and Paul took charge of the tomato sauce, which included fresh basil from the herb garden. We worked on that meal for hours. While we cooked, Paul told John and me the story of the first time he ever tried pizza. "It was a totally unfamiliar, foreign food, but when a pizzeria opened near my house in Chicago, I was dying to try it. I convinced a few friends of mine to go over there, and it felt kind of dangerous. One of my friends in particular was terrified, and when he looked back into the kitchen to see the pizza chef scratching his lower back he lost it—'Look!' he said, 'He's picking his butt and then cooking the food! Let's get out of here.' We talked him down and stayed. It was absolutely delicious." Even Paul Strohm had to get out of the house and out of his comfort zone as a teenager in order to become the eventual epitome of coolness.

Our pizzas were delicious too, and family and friends were amazed that we'd made every single component from scratch. That's the last meal I remember having at the Strohm's before John left Bloomington for Berklee, and I soon followed him out to Boston. I took the hours I'd spent in that house with me; they had permanently shaped my taste in music and my appreciation for food. It must have been annoying for my mother to endure those insensitive dinner table comparisons. Sorry, Mom. Be comforted by this: I think I know now how it must have felt.

"Jacob's dad puts something in his eggs," said Jonah. Sigh. My teenager was sitting at the breakfast table in Evanston, but his heart was still back in Bloomington with his childhood friend. Jonah had been hanging out at Jacob's place since they were both four-year-olds, and he had always loved it. The house is big and open, right on the edge of a forest, surrounded by stunning vegetable gardens, and full of cats and dogs. Full of musical instruments, too—everybody in that family plays something, and they often spend evenings jamming in the living room, with Jacob on mandolin, his sister on bass, and father on guitar. When Jonah visits them, he joins in sometimes on keyboard. We love music in our family, and most of us are musicians too, but playing together is not part of our family's scene. It warmed my heart to think of Jonah sharing these cozy episodes. I knew it was formative for him, was bringing qualities to his life that his father and I didn't have to offer. I have always wanted this experience of other people's homes for him. I wouldn't be who I am without that memorable first stir-fry, those startling early R.E.M. songs. We all need to get outside of our little nuclear family circles.

But still. I was irritated about the scrambled eggs. The rice was bothering me too. I called Jacob's dad. "OK," I said, trying to keep the hostility out of my voice. "What do you put in your rice that's so great?"

"I never cook it in plain water. I add in a little broth."

Oh. That struck me as a good idea. I made a mental note to try that myself.

"And what about your scrambled eggs?"

"I make my own chili powder," he said. "It's no big deal, I just dry an assortment of peppers from my garden and grind them together."

I couldn't compete with that. But what I *could* do is teach Jonah how to make a great stir-fry. A month of stir-fry lessons was also an easy and natural extension of our vegan month. For the next few weeks we peeled ginger, whisked sauces, chopped vegetables. We heated oil (coconut, which can also take the heat) and added first the hard vegetables, then the softer ones, into my beat-up wok. After a few tries, Jonah had another culinary skill in his pocket. I predict that he will make a lot of stir-fries in his life. As far as how to make amazing scrambled eggs, I'll leave that lesson to Jacob's dad.

Sweet and Spicy Vermicelli Stir-Fry

I know it seems weird to use regular Italian-style vermicelli in a stir-fry, but it works really well. I discovered this by accident when I asked Jake to buy rice vermicelli and he brought home a box of wheat pasta instead. We all immediately loved it. You can certainly substitute rice noodles here, or any noodle—udon noodles would also be great.

Serves 4–6

1 8-ounce box vermicelli, or other noodle

4 tablespoons soy sauce

2 tablespoons cooking sherry

1 heaping tablespoon cornstarch

1 tablespoon brown sugar

Big pinch ground cayenne pepper

2 tablespoons coconut or peanut oil

1 small head cabbage, cored and thinly sliced (approximately 4 cups)

1 pound mushrooms, any kind, thinly sliced

1 red bell pepper, thinly sliced

3 cloves garlic, minced

4 green onions, thinly sliced

Hot pepper sesame oil for serving, optional but highly recommended!

1.   Cook the noodles according to package directions. Drain and set aside.

2.   Make sure all the prepared vegetables are close at hand. In a small bowl, whisk together ½ cup of water with the soy sauce, sherry, cornstarch, brown sugar, and cayenne to create a sauce. Set aside.

3.   Heat a wok over high heat. The wok is ready when a drop of water flung onto its surface evaporates immediately.

RECIPE CONTINUES

4. Add the oil and swirl the wok around to coat completely. Add the cabbage and cook, stirring continuously, for 1 minute. Add the mushrooms and pepper and stir for 3 to 4 minutes. Add the garlic and cook, still stirring continuous, for another minute. Add the sauce and noodles. Stir well to combine and to thicken the sauce, 3 to 4 minutes. Add the green onions, stir well, and remove from the heat.

5. Serve immediately, piping hot, topped with optional hot pepper sesame oil, if using.

Mushroom and Kale Stir-Fry

You gotta love mushrooms for this one. And you really need a wok, or a HUGE skillet. Any mushrooms can work—I like a combination of field mushrooms and shiitakes. Make sure to complete all your prep work before you start cooking. You want everything ready and close at hand— once you begin it's all very fast and furious!

Serves 4

6–8 ounces ramen noodles, optional

4 tablespoons soy sauce

2 tablespoons mirin, cooking sherry, or dry white wine

1 tablespoon hot pepper sesame oil or 1 tablespoon toasted sesame oil plus a nice big pinch of ground cayenne pepper

1 heaping tablespoon cornstarch

2 tablespoons minced fresh ginger or 1 teaspoon ground ginger

2 tablespoons coconut or peanut oil

2 medium bunches kale, washed, stems removed and discarded, leaves chopped

1½ pounds mushrooms, sliced, stems removed and discarded

2–3 cloves garlic, minced

Sea salt, to taste, optional

Hot pepper sesame oil for garnish, optional

Toasted sesame seeds for garnish, optional

1. If you are using the ramen noodles, cook according to the package directions and then set aside.

2. In a small bowl, whisk together the soy sauce, mirin, sesame oil, cornstarch, ground ginger (if you are using fresh ginger instead, you will add it later) and ½ cup of water. Set aside.

3. Heat a wok over high heat—the wok is ready when a drop of water flung onto its surface evaporates immediately.

RECIPE CONTINUES

4. Add the coconut or peanut oil and heat for a few seconds before adding the kale a few big handfuls at a time. Stir constantly. If the kale begins to burn, reduce the heat a bit. Once all the kale is added, stir-fry for about 3 more minutes, or until kale is almost tender. Add a little water if the kale is sticking to the wok.

5. Add the mushrooms and stir continuously for about 3 minutes, or until the mushrooms shrink and start to brown.

6. Push the kale and mushrooms to one side of the wok (this will slow the cooking process, as the middle is the hottest part of the wok), and add the garlic and fresh ginger (if using) to the middle. Cook the garlic and ginger in the middle of the wok for a few seconds, stirring constantly, then stir everything together to combine.

7. Quickly whisk the prepared sauce and then pour it down the side of the wok (don't pour it in the middle; it will cool the wok down and might make your stir-fry soggy, yuck). Stir constantly for about 2 minutes, or until the sauce thickens and coats everything.

8. Taste and adjust seasoning as needed. Add a little salt to taste. If you're having this with ramen noodles, add them to the wok and stir to combine. Garnish with hot pepper sesame oil and sesame seeds, if you wish. Eat immediately. I can vouch for the leftovers.

Greens with Peanut–Ginger Sauce

I made this up one Sunday night when I realized we hadn't eaten any vegetables all weekend. It's a great way to catch up on your greens. Good with rice or noodles, but also a fine, simple meal on its own. One tester pointed out that this is a little low in protein to be a main dish—you might add baked tempeh or tofu to make it more sustaining.

Serves 2, doubles well

3 inches fresh ginger root

2 medium or 3 small bunches greens, such as a mixture of collard greens and kale, stems removed and discarded

3 tablespoons smooth, unsalted peanut butter

2 tablespoons soy sauce

2 teaspoons garlic chili hot sauce

2 tablespoons coconut or peanut oil

2 cloves garlic, minced as finely as possible

1 scallion, sliced, optional

1. Grate the ginger root, gather it into a ball, and squeeze to extract the juice. Set aside 1 tablespoon of ginger juice (you can discard the rest or reserve for another use).

2. Stack the greens, roll them up tightly like a cigar, and slice width-wise. Set aside.

3. Heat ⅓ cup water and set aside. The water should be very hot, but not boiling.

4. In a small bowl, use a fork to mash together peanut butter, soy sauce, hot sauce, and ginger juice. Add a little hot water and whisk to blend well. Whisk in the remaining water. Set aside.

RECIPE CONTINUES

5.   Heat a wok or big skillet over high heat. The wok is ready when a drop of water flung onto its surface evaporates immediately. Add the oil and swirl to coat. Add greens, in batches if necessary, and stir-fry (cook, stirring continuously) 3 to 4 minutes. Add the garlic and stir-fry for 1 minute. Add the prepared sauce, stir well, and cook for 1 minute more.

6.   Serve immediately, with optional scallion sprinkled on top, and with extra garlic chili hot sauce if you like.

CHAPTER FIVE

Macaroni and Cheese and Other Road Food

ONE-AND-A-HALF POUNDS OF CHEESE, four cups of whole milk, nearly a stick of butter, two large eggs, a pound of macaroni. The list of main ingredients was short, but the quantities of each, piled together on our kitchen countertop, were impressive. "We are going to dairy hell," said Jonah. He sounded sincerely happy about it.

Our vegan month of beans and our wok-heavy month of vegetable stir-fries seemed to fade into the past. It was impossible to consider a year of cooking lessons with Jonah that excluded his lifelong favorite meal: macaroni and cheese. When is macaroni and cheese more than macaroni and cheese? The answer might be always. When Jonah was a toddler, I'd battled pangs of guilt about how much of it he ate. He loved the kind that came in a box with a packet of dried cheese powder. He loved the kind that came in a frozen block, and always took too long to heat, so you'd inevitably crunch into a little icy patch in the middle. And most of all he loved the deep casserole dish of the homemade variety that I made on occasion, and of which there were never leftovers. To assuage the guilt, I served it with a big side of steamed broccoli.

I felt fresh pangs of guilt about our descent into dairy hell. We'd been eating well and I wanted to encourage Jonah to keep up his wholesome new habits. I wanted to model discipline and demonstrate smart choices. I considered teaching him how to make my vegan answer to mac and cheese, a butternut squash ziti I'd developed over the years. But I didn't want to model rigidity. During a stretch of time in my early twenties, I adopted an extremely low-fat version of my already-vegetarian diet (does anybody remember Pritikin?). I stuck to it ruthlessly. I will forever cringe when I recall a lovingly prepared fettuccine Alfredo I refused to eat at a friend's house, insisting instead on a plate of plain pasta sprinkled with black pepper. I didn't want my kids to resemble *that* crazy bitch. That friend never invited me to dinner again. Maybe we shouldn't eat macaroni and cheese for dinner every night, but—with all respectful allowances for allergies, intolerance, and ethical objections to animal food—it is always a good idea to feed your soul a bit of what it fancies. Jonah fancies mac and cheese.

Being a musician on tour was the life experience that shattered my uptightness and helped me embrace a more flexible diet. Touring in a band presents a host of particular challenges: how to stay stable in constantly shifting surroundings; how to stay sane in often-crazy circumstances; how to stay civil in the close quarters of a van with four other humans; how to stay healthy in booze and smoke-filled bars—and on the slim pickings of truckstop food. It didn't take me long to discover that food was key to everything—stability, sanity, civility, and health—and plain pasta would not cut it. I sought out restaurants with good-quality vegetarian food. I didn't always find them (it was harder pre-Internet!), and so I learned to relax and do the best I could. Over many, many years, my map of America was drawn out of small rock clubs and reliable vegetarian-friendly restaurants. The Knitting Factory and Angelica Kitchen in New York. The Blind Pig and Seva in Ann Arbor. The Crocodile Café and the Gravity Bar in Seattle. The Middle East and the Five Seasons in Boston. But of all the bars and restaurants in all the towns in all the world, there is none that compares to the 40-Watt and The Grit in Athens, Georgia

Athens is a town that outshines all the others in my memory. In part, it's because I rolled through there during a few pivotal moments in my life. The first visit, all the way back in 1988, shines the brightest. It was during the first Blake Babies tour, a ramshackle effort along the East Coast and down into Georgia. We were already on our third line-up: me on drums, John on lead guitar, Juliana playing rhythm guitar and singing lead, and Evan Dando, on loan from up-and-coming Boston punk band the Lemonheads, on bass and backing vocals. The Blake Babies and the Lemonheads had formed in Boston at about the same time, discovered each other quickly, and become fast friends.

Evan and his Lemonheads partner, guitarist/singer/songwriter Ben Deily, attended one of the first shows the Blake Babies ever played, at an arty café called "She's Leaving Home." Evan stood front and center, enthusiastically rocking out, and Juliana was smitten from that moment and far into the future. Of course, it was hard to meet that golden boy and *not* be smitten. Few people will ever gaze upon a human more beautiful than 19-year-old Evan Dando. And Evan wasn't just a pretty face—he was an uncanny talent, with a killer voice, a knack for melody, and great taste in music. I will love him forever for bringing his copy of Big

Star's *Radio City* over to the apartment I shared with John and Juliana. "You guys are going to freak out," he said. "I promise." He was right. When Evan agreed to join the Blake Babies after we had unsuccessfully worked with two other bass players, we were delighted. As it turned out, it was only the beginning of a long cross-pollination between the two bands. John would later join the Lemonheads on drums, and years after that he would return as a guitar player. After the Blake Babies broke up, Juliana was an integral part of the Lemonheads' classic record, *It's a Shame About Ray.*

Evan and Juliana's rock stardom and tour buses were a long way in the future from that first Blake Babies tour. We travelled in Evan's white station wagon, a hand-me-down from his dad. Shows were booked and the trip stitched together by a generous friend and early fan of the band, Michael Wegner, a recent transplant to Athens from Providence, Rhode Island. We were deliriously happy to be on tour; we didn't care that we played one night in front of two friends (including Michael) and a confused promoter (who later said to John, "You need to get those girls in some dresses"). We loved everything about touring. We loved truck stops, where we bought *Penthouse* and persuaded Juliana to read the "Forum" section out loud to help pass the time on long drives. We loved Waffle House, where we became obsessed with the Waffle House theme song to such an extent that we taped it on our boom box so we could listen to it whenever we wanted. Which turned out to be often. When we played with They Might Be Giants, we were disappointed that they weren't as excited by the Waffle House theme song as we were. Nobody on earth was as excited about anything as we were about everything. I even enjoyed hauling gear, and noticed that by the end of the trip my arm muscles were becoming more pronounced.

"Hey," I said to Juliana, lugging my heavy bass drum to the station wagon. "Touring is making me fit! Isn't that cool?"

We might have been slightly irritating to be around.

Every stop along the road was amazing, but when we arrived in Athens, I thought we'd hit Shangri-La. Everybody feels this sometimes, right? You're visiting a town, you fall under its spell, and you ask yourself, "Could I live here?" There are other questions embedded in this one like, "Would my life be different and better—would *I* be different and better—if I lived here?" Athens inspired me to ask these questions. And it wasn't one particular thing about the place, it was everything: the draping kudzu, the warm sweet air, and the population of pretty boys, all of them into poetry. We stayed with Michael in an old, slightly damp, undeniably charming house that he shared with Lynda Stipe, another musician and the sister of R.E.M. singer Michael. This was a detail that dazzled me, John, Juliana, and Evan, though we tried to play it cool. Every gesture by every citizen of Athens seemed to be an artistic statement. In Michael and Lynda's house, autumn leaves covered the kitchen floor, leaves they swept in deliberately for the pleasure of that underfoot crunch.

And then there was the club, the 40-Watt, an otherwise standard venue that shimmered with the traces of its venerable history. Amazing bands had launched from its stage—the B-52s, Pylon, and of course R.E.M. I imagined I could feel their presence. Our show there went well. Thanks to Michael's vigilant efforts at promotion, we drew a small but respectably sized crowd. During our set I looked out to see Lynda Stipe and her boyfriend ballroom dancing boisterously across the floor. The next morning, in her kitchen among the autumn leaves, she offered her review of the show: "Y'all's music is hard to waltz to." Oh well. Nothing could make me love Athens less. I had fallen for the place.

The meals I ate during those few days made me fall even harder. Even the restaurants in Athens were quirky and creative, every plate of food lovingly prepared and determinedly non-mainstream, from soul food (butter beans, greens, and cornbread) served cafeteria-style to the grainy, delicious whole wheat biscuits at the Bluebird Café, to well, *everything* at The Grit.

Which brings me to The Grit: a fantastic vegetarian restaurant and a central Athens hangout, a place I'd come to anticipate visiting for years and tours to come. Food at The Grit was simple and distinctive. During that first visit, I had a bowl of brown rice, pinto beans, and vegetables that was *exciting*. Now I recognize that the excitement had a lot to do with the fact that The Grit, and that bowl of rice and beans, resided in the heart of a *scene,* a creative community in the process of inventing itself, realizing itself. Athens made it seem like any place in the world could become an artistic center, not just New York, Paris, or London, and like anybody could be an artist, whether they came from a family of painters, farmers, or factory workers.

The Blake Babies seemed to fit right in. We were on this tour to promote our first record, *Nicely, Nicely*, which we had recorded piecemeal: some in a recording studio, some at a live gig at Harvard University. We'd received help from dozens of people to make the record happen. Parents donated money, friends volunteered time and effort and microphones, fellow musicians doled out advice and instructions. We tried for a while to find a record label, making a cassette demo and sending it around, but when nobody called us back, we forged ahead and put it out on our own label, which we called Chewbud Records. The cover art for *Nicely, Nicely* featured the slightly crazy, adorable doodles that covered Juliana's notebooks, and the back of the album featured unprofessional, unguarded photos of us in our shared apartment. It was DIY at every level. When the record came out, we packaged up copies and sent them to radio stations and zines using a list generously shared by Curtis Casella from Taang! Records, the Lemonheads' first label.

And the DIY didn't stop there. We waited impatiently for radio stations to play the record, and when it didn't happen to our satisfaction, we made it happen. One night, we shamelessly called Emerson College's WERS and requested the song we'd decided was the single, "Wipe it Up," during the station's local radio show. It was a sweet moment of triumph, sitting in our living room, hearing our song over the airwaves.

During the entire *Nicely, Nicely* promotion cycle, including the station wagon tour, we had our eyes on bigger prizes—we wanted a real record label, agent, manager, all the things bands are supposed to want. But we must have known somewhere in the backs of our minds that this was a golden age for us, and that once we surrendered aspects of our career to others, we'd lose some of this glowing "go, team" feeling.

In Athens, I could see the lines connecting the dots from the leaves on Lynda Stipe's floor, to the doodles on our album cover, to the homely and delicious bowl of rice and beans at The Grit. The lines added up to a picture full of possibility. I wish I could say that subsequent tours were as joyful as that first jaunt. Touring became a little less fun, and then a lot less fun, but I was lucky to be able to return to Athens many times, and regardless of whatever else was going on, I always enjoyed breathing its air and eating its food.

My next pivotal moment in Athens came a few years later, during the last extensive stretch of Blake Babies touring before we broke up. What a difference from that first giddy tour. Internally, our musical visions for the band were diverging. Juliana was listening to more Wilson Philips; John and I were listening to more Spacemen 3. It can't have been much fun for Juliana to be in a band with an on-again-off-again couple, either. Externally, our record label, Mammoth, had expectations that cast a shadow over us. We never seemed to live up to their hopes. While we had jumped up and down in our living room over one single radio play on WERS, Mammoth seemed frustrated with our lack of radio play. The high-profile showcases that the label organized never seemed to go as well as they'd hoped. As the pressure on us increased, our happiness and satisfaction decreased. Of course, this is a transition that most successful bands must make, and many make it smoothly. We didn't. I must admit that I personally went from wide-eyed and appreciative to mildly entitled. After a series of tours opening up for bands like the Chills, the Connells, and Buffalo Tom, playing in nice venues, I grew accustomed to certain comforts. At one show, opening for fIREHOSE, I complained to Mike Watt that the venue had no backstage dressing room.

"What do you need a backstage room for?" asked Watt.

"Well," I said petulantly, "I need some place to sit down."

"Freda," said Watt, with a big smile, "there's plenty of chairs here." He spread his arms wide to the main room, full indeed of tables and chairs. Mike Watt. Forever punk. Forever doing it for the right reasons.

Tension in the band increased more when a major producer, David Kahne, began to court Juliana. He had recently worked with the Bangles and successfully persuaded Susanna Hoffs to leave that band behind and embark on a solo career. Not surprisingly, he had minimal interest in John and even less interest in me. As the band grew a little more popular, it was clear that one Blake Baby had star power and the possibility of a major career. I'd known all along that there was something very special about Juliana, and I wasn't surprised when the world caught on. And I would never, ever blame her for wanting to strike out on her own. But all of this was a strain as the band kept plugging away. We were fed up with each other and bickering too much.

In the middle of this tour, we had decided to break up but continued going through the motions of playing shows. I must have seen it coming. I had already packed my bags and left Boston, and was living with my father and stepmom in Indianapolis. Or rather, I was mostly just storing my stuff in their house throughout the interminable touring. I was depressed, felt lost, and on top of everything, things were bad between me and John. We should have been broken up completely by then. We'd grown apart in many ways, yet the long-term bond we'd forged as high-schoolers was tough to dissolve.

At the same time, the first Gulf War was raging. I was glad to be back in Athens. I hoped its magic would sooth my soul. During our day there, I spent time on my own, walking around my favorite town; it was as charming as ever. I came upon an extensive shantytown of mostly University of Georgia student protestors. They were smart and earnest, insistent that their makeshift village would stand and promote dialogue until the war ended.

As I talked to the protestors, I kind of wished I were one of them. I was the same age, after all, but instead of going to college I'd been devoted to the band. Hanging out in that shantytown was a nice break from the by-then-routine grind of hanging out in rock clubs with musicians. My old love of Athens swelled within me. *I really should move here*, I thought. My band was breaking up. My relationship was falling apart. I was only 22. I could do whatever I wanted. The thought cheered me a little, and helped me to survive the remainder of that long and brutal tour. I was serious about moving to Athens, but my plans changed when, very soon after that trip, I met and fell in love with an amazing bass player named Jake Smith back in Indiana. Athens was destined to be one of my roads not taken.

But the road has led me back there, periodically. My most recent trip to Athens was almost ten years later. The Blake Babies had reunited for an album and tour in 2001, characterized by genuine good will and a desire to reconnect to those earlier days when we felt lucky, hopeful, and energized. We were older and wiser Blake Babies, and much had changed in all of our lives. Juliana had become an established singer/songwriter. John had continued playing music and making records, had toured extensively with the Lemonheads, and was just about to get married and begin law school. I'd married that amazing bass player; we had settled down in Bloomington with our two sons and formed the Mysteries of Life. I was finally almost finished with my undergraduate degree. Jake was starting graduate school. The Blake Babies reunion tour was my first extended absence from the family: I'd left seven-year-old Jonah and two-and-a-half year-old Henry at home with Jake. I had mixed feelings about it, but a strong desire to balance what I hoped was a renewed career in music with motherhood and marriage.

The reality was complicated. I felt light and free away from the daily demands of motherhood—waking in a bed alone, absolved from preparing meals or orchestrating the school run, happy to focus on music and have a little time to myself. I also felt, at moments, a visceral panic unlike anything I've ever experienced, with pangs of grief and a longing that defied logic. Pure animal stuff. And later, back home, I'd encounter surprise attacks, as fellow preschool moms—ones I didn't know very well—would say, "I think it's *great* that you can leave your kids like that for so long. I could *never* do that."

"Yes," I would say, my eyes stinging, "it's great."

The Blake Babies reunion tour was quick, jam-packed, fun, and successful. Old friends popped up at every stop, which helped me sail through the tough moments. I was thrilled to return to Athens and couldn't wait to eat at The Grit. Athens had changed. It was tidy, more developed, and felt well on the other side of its process of invention and realization. The Grit had changed, too, right in step with the town. The restaurant had moved into a spiffy new building and although you could still order a bowl of rice and beans, there were new and more elegant options on the menu. I ordered tempeh tetrazzini and a piece of blueberry pie. Gentrification had not diminished the quality of the food. The tempeh dish was a dream come true for a vegetarian on the road:

high-protein, savory, and satisfying. Eating well on the road was much easier in 2001 than it had been in 1988, but The Grit was still head and shoulders above what you could find in most towns.

Then I ate the pie. And that piece of pie made me quietly break down and cry. It was not just good, it was perfect. Was I simply awash in hormones, missing my family, reminded by that pie of home and domesticity? Or was it Athens, doing that thing that it does, despite its cleaned-up appearance, still draped in kudzu and mystery, my forever road not taken? I don't know. But I cried real tears all over that piece of blueberry pie and then I ate it all, every crumb. And I felt much better.

I haven't been back to The Grit since then and hadn't thought about it much until recently, when Jake gave me *The Grit Restaurant Cookbook* as a birthday present. "The Grit!" I said. "Oh my God I loved that place." I immediately turned to the dessert section and there it was—Blueberry Pie. I flipped through the book, reading the endorsements from musicians that were woven among the recipes. Singer-songwriter Masha writes, "There is so much love inside The Grit we believe there is going to be an explosion." Marc Perlman from the Jayhawks writes, "When on tour, we usually don't get up until we've already ridden out of town. Hence we never eat until the next town. Unless we're in Athens, then we set our alarms and get our asses out of bed—or just stay up all night. All because of The Grit. We're all about The Grit." I clearly wasn't the only one. I found all the old familiar foods—tempeh tetrazzini, Grit Pintos. Then something even more familiar: testimonials from my Blake Babies band mates, John and Juliana. I felt my entire life shrink and collapse onto the pages of a cookbook.

In the kitchen with Jonah, nary an autumn leaf underfoot, we dove into our cooking lesson. I had a cookbook open on the counter—you guessed it, *The Grit Restaurant Cookbook*. I'd found more than traces of my personal history in this cookbook; I'd also found a perfect recipe for macaroni and cheese. Jonah was seventeen, less than two years younger than I'd been when Lynda Stipe tried fruitlessly to waltz to my drumming. While we cooked, I brought up the subject of Athens and touring with Jonah, and he listened politely as I recounted these experiences. I hadn't talked much with my kids about my rock life, and they always seem momentarily surprised and impressed during these rare conversations, like when Jonah discovered the Pixies and asked me if I'd ever heard them. "I've played tons of gigs with the Pixies," I said, sighing, irrationally exasperated that he knew so little about me (with only myself to blame for never bringing it up). "I shared a rehearsal space in Boston with the Pixies." And then, growing a bit shrill, "I played Euchre with the Pixies!" I recalled a night in Los Angeles after a Blake Babies gig, when we connected with our friends in the Boston punk band Bullet LaVolta. LaVolta and the Pixies were recording in neighboring studios at the time, and they'd been hanging out together. Members of all three bands gathered for an impromptu late-night party, the kind that rarely happened with the Blake Babies. We were a fairly nerdy troupe, and gigs were usually followed by a sandwich, a good book, and a cup of Sleepytime Herbal Tea. But once in a while we partied like rock stars. Much of that Los Angeles night is a whiskey-tinged blur, but I recall a hotel apartment, loud music, and exuberant conversation, and cards around a table with LaVolta drummer Todd Philips, singer Yukki Gipe, and Pixies bassist (and coolest person in the world) Kim Deal.

"Wow," Jonah said. "Cool."

Yes. But if I was ever cool (I wasn't—not like Kim Deal—but whatever), I certainly wasn't anymore, least of all in the eyes of my kids. Mostly I didn't care, but sometimes it could be disorienting to reconcile Rock Me with Mom Me. Those tours away from my little kids had been difficult, and not just because of the wounding comments from the other preschool moms. But the difficulty had been worth it—those times represented one of the rare periods in my life when my identity felt full and complete rather than fractured and disjointed.

I wondered, *should I have tried harder to keep that part of me alive? And was it too late? Might I have another chance to be a mother and an artist?* That possibility felt far, far away from me then. I was temping in an academic office in Evanston, a city that still felt new and foreign. I hadn't played a show in years. I was writing a little, but the most creative thing I was doing was teaching my son how to cook. But the act of teaching Jonah how to make macaroni and cheese, and remembering and telling stories of my past, was breathing new life into that neglected corner of my identity.

The homemade macaroni and cheese I'd cooked for toddler Jonah had been made from a roux-based white sauce, and it was always good, but once I tried The Grit's richer, egg-thickened sauce I couldn't go back to even the faintest taste of flour. Plain-Pasta-Eating Freda would not have tasted a single spoonful of what Jonah and I were cooking up. Thankfully, she's not around anymore. Rock tours and family life have demanded flexibility, and so I spare Jonah all lectures about fat, cholesterol, refined pasta, and the evils of dairy. Instead, I show him that eggs can thicken a sauce, and that long patient stirring is relaxing and rewarding. I remind him that his mom was a drummer in rock bands, and I share with him the power of food and memory. I teach him this: If you want to make a hungry family or starving rock band sigh with delight; if you want to see some people you're feeding loosen their belts and clean their plates; then you can't go wrong with a rich creamy sauce, a kick of mustard and cayenne, and brown buttery breadcrumbs. If it makes you feel better, serve it with a side of broccoli.

Macaroni and Cheese

Adapted from *The Grit Restaurant Cookbook*. "The most heavenly mac and cheese," said one of my testers. I have nothing to add to that. Use whatever cheese you like; I prefer a mixture of sharp and mild cheddar.

Makes enough to feed a 6-piece band or family

1 pound macaroni

6 tablespoons salted butter, divided, plus more for greasing

2 large eggs

4 cups whole milk

1 tablespoon dijon mustard

2 teaspoons salt, plus more for cooking

Large pinch freshly ground black pepper

Large pinch ground cayenne pepper

1½ pounds cheddar cheese or any other cheese, grated

1½ cups panko breadcrumbs

1. Preheat the oven to 425°F. Grease a 9 × 13-inch casserole dish with butter and set aside.

2. Bring a large pot of water to a rolling boil, add a generous pinch of salt, and cook the macaroni until it is al dente or even more undercooked, about 5 or 6 minutes. Remove and drain. Put the empty pot back on the stove and melt 3 tablespoons of the butter over medium heat. Add the cooked pasta back in and stir well to combine. Remove from the heat and set aside.

3. In a medium bowl, whisk together the eggs, milk, mustard, salt, pepper, and cayenne. Add this mixture to the pasta and stir well. Add the cheese and stir constantly over medium-high heat, until the cheese melts and the sauce thickens. This takes a while, at least 10 to 15 minutes. Keep cooking and stirring until it gets very thick and creamy—I promise it will happen eventually—and then pour into the prepared casserole and set aside.

4. In a small saucepan, melt the remaining 3 tablespoons of the butter and add the panko, stirring well to coat with the butter. Spread this mixture over the top of macaroni and bake for 15 minutes. I like to broil the dish for 1 minute at the end to make it very brown and crispy on top. Serve immediately.

Butternut Squash Ziti

Mock dishes make sad faces. Remember that carob brownie you bit into so eagerly, only to be crushed with disappointment? I used to make this dish with elbow macaroni topped with breadcrumbs, and it met with a lukewarm reception. When I switched to ziti and ditched the bread-crumbs, the dish no longer seemed to be passing itself off as macaroni and cheese, and everybody suddenly liked it. This is a nice one for the vegans at your next potluck.

Serves 8–10

1 large (3¾–4-pound) butternut squash

1 pound ziti or penne

¼ cup olive oil, plus more for greasing

1 medium yellow onion, very finely chopped

2 teaspoons plus pinch salt, divided

3 medium cloves garlic, minced

1 teaspoon dried thyme

½ teaspoon dried sage

¼ teaspoon ground white pepper

Big pinch ground cayenne pepper

¼ cup unbleached flour

1 cup unsweetened soy or almond milk

1 14-ounce can unsweetened, full-fat coconut milk

1.   Preheat the oven to 375°F. Lightly grease a 9 × 11-inch casserole dish with olive oil and set aside.

2.   Line a baking sheet with parchment paper. Halve the squash lengthwise (keep the seeds intact) and place face-down on the prepared sheet. Bake for 1 to 1½ hours, or until easily pierced with a knife and juices are slightly bubbling. Remove from the oven and let cool. Once cool to the touch, remove and discard the seeds and pulp. Remove and discard the skin. In a food pro-cessor or blender, purée about ½ of the squash (keep the un-puréed squash for a later step). Set aside.

3. Cook the pasta according to package directions; drain, rinse with cold water, and set aside.

4. In a large, heavy pot over medium-low heat, warm the olive oil. Add the onion and a pinch of salt and cook until very soft, sweet, and slightly golden, at least 15 minutes. Add the garlic and continue to cook, stirring frequently, for an additional 1 to 2 minutes. Stir in the 2 teaspoons of salt along with the thyme, sage, white pepper, and cayenne pepper.

5. Add the flour and continue to cook over medium-low heat, stirring constantly, until the flour smells nutty and toasty, about 5 minutes. Whisk in the soy or almond milk. Whisk in 1 cup of water, about ½ cup at a time, then whisk in the coconut milk. Bring the mixture to a simmer and stir constantly until the sauce begins to thicken.

6. Add the puréed squash and stir well. Using a spoon, scoop bite-sized pieces of the un-puréed squash into the sauce (I like the look and texture of this dish best when it's not all smooth—the chunks of squash add interest). Let simmer for about 15 minutes, stirring often. Taste and adjust seasoning as needed.

7. Add the cooked pasta to the pot and stir well to combine. Transfer the mixture to the prepared casserole dish and bake 15 to 20 minutes. Let cool a few minutes before serving.

Tempeh Tetrazzini

Adapted from a recipe in *The Grit Restaurant Cookbook*. The original includes a mixture of celery, carrots, and peas that was not a hit with my family. Henry suggested broccoli, and the substitution stuck. I also increased the amounts of mustard and Worcestershire sauce after a tester suggested giving the recipe more of a kick.

Serves 6–8

For the Sauce

6 tablespoons unsalted butter or olive oil

6 tablespoons all-purpose flour

4¼ cups milk or unsweetened soy milk, divided

1 tablespoon soy sauce

1 heaping teaspoon salt

1 teaspoon Dijon mustard

Big pinch freshly ground black pepper

Big pinch ground cayenne pepper

¼ cup white wine or fresh lemon juice

For the Tempeh

2 tablespoons butter or olive oil

1 small onion, finely chopped

1 8-ounce package tempeh, chopped into ¼-inch cubes

3 tablespoons Worcestershire sauce

2 tablespoons soy sauce

8 ounces mushrooms, finely chopped

3 cloves garlic, minced

For Assembly

2 pounds broccoli, cut into small florets

8 ounces egg noodles or "egg-free" noodles

6 ounces smoked Gouda cheese or other cheese (or any vegan smoked-cheese substitute), shredded

1 heaping cup panko breadcrumbs

To Make the Sauce

1. In a 2-quart, heavy-bottomed saucepan over medium heat, melt the butter (or warm the oil). Stir in the flour and bring to a slight bubble. Stir constantly for 2 to 3 minutes, until flour smells slightly toasty. Do not brown. Whisk in 2 cups of the milk or soy milk. Whisking constantly, increase the heat to bring to bubbling.

2. Add the soy sauce, salt, mustard, pepper, and cayenne pepper. When the mixture is thick, slowly add the remaining 2¼ cups of milk, about ½ cup at a time, and cook until thick and bubbling. Stir in the wine or lemon juice. Taste and adjust the seasoning as needed. Remove from the heat and set aside.

To Make the Tempeh

1. In a large skillet over medium-high heat, melt the butter (or warm the oil). Add the onion and cook, stirring frequently, for 5 to 6 minutes. Add the tempeh and stir well. Add the Worcestershire and soy sauce and stir for 5 more minutes to brown the tempeh and onions. Add the mushrooms and garlic and stir for 5 additional minutes or so, until the mushrooms are tender. Remove from the heat and set aside.

To Assemble

1. Cook the noodles al dente, according to package instructions. Add the broccoli in last 2 minutes of cooking. Drain well and set aside.

RECIPE CONTINUES

2. Preheat the oven to 375°F. Grease a 9 × 13-inch casserole dish.

3. Layer the ingredients into the prepared casserole this order: 1 cup of the sauce, ½ of the tempeh mixture, ½ of the cheese, all of the noodles and broccoli, 2 cups of the sauce, the remaining ½ tempeh mixture, the remaining cheese, then the remaining sauce. Top with the panko to completely cover the casserole. Press down lightly onto the panko.

4. Bake for 40 minutes, until the edges are bubbling and the panko is very brown. You can broil for a couple of minutes at the end if you need to. Let cool for 10 minutes before serving.

Blueberry Pie

Adapted from a recipe in *The Grit Restaurant Cookbook*—I decreased the sugar and upped the lemon juice to rebalance the flavors. "A grand-slam home run," wrote one tester.

Plan ahead—this needs to sit in the refrigerator overnight in order to become truly amazing.

I did not include a dough recipe, figuring everyone has a favorite already. I always use the *Cook's Illustrated* Foolproof Pie Dough recipe. You can also purchase pre-made frozen dough.

Makes one 9-inch pie

Oil, for greasing

Double-crust pie dough

2 tablespoons cornstarch

Juice and zest of 1 medium lemon

2 teaspoons vanilla extract

2 teaspoons brandy

4½ cups fresh blueberries

¾ cup granulated sugar

2 tablespoons salted butter, chopped into small pieces

1 heaping tablespoon sour cream

1 tablespoon all-purpose flour

¼ teaspoon ground cinnamon

1. Preheat the oven to 450°F. Lightly grease a deep, 9-inch pie pan.

2. Roll out ½ of the dough and transfer it to the prepared pan, pressing lightly and evenly into the bottom and sides.

3. In a large bowl, combine the cornstarch, lemon juice and zest, vanilla, and brandy and mix well. Add the blueberries, sugar, butter, sour cream, flour, and cinnamon and gently stir until combined. Pour the mixture into the prepared pie crust.

RECIPE CONTINUES

4. Roll out the remaining ½ of the dough. Cover the pie with the dough trimming as needed. Crimp to seal the edge of the pie. Prick or slash the top in whatever pattern you fancy, to allow steam to escape.

5. Place the pie on a large cookie sheet lined with parchment paper. (This is really important! This is a very juicy pie that will otherwise drip all over your oven!) Bake for 10 minutes, then reduce the oven heat to 350°F and bake an additional 50 to 55 minutes, until golden and bubbling. Remove from the oven and let cool to room temperature. Cover and refrigerate overnight. Yes, overnight. Your patience will be rewarded. Pairs very well with ice cream.

CHAPTER SIX

Home Fires Burning

WE PEELED POTATOES, pushed them through the food processor into thin slices, buttered a baking dish and layered the slices in, sprinkled them with plenty of salt and pepper, then added garlic and chunks of vegetarian sausage, poured cream over the whole thing, and baked it until the potatoes melted into the cream. And then into our mouths.

We centered four white tilapia fillets on squares of aluminum foil and topped each with a blob of well-seasoned butter—Worcestershire sauce, paprika, garlic, salt, pepper. We sealed the edges of the foil, creating airtight pouches around the fish. When it was done we slid the hot foil packs onto plates and served immediately. The fish was so tender it fell apart at the touch of our forks, wafting fragrant steam up into our faces.

We sautéed minced onions, cashews, and garlic, stirred in cooked rice and lentils, seasoned the mixture with basil and thyme, and stuffed it into big portobello caps. We took them out of the oven when the stuffing was crispy and brown and the mushrooms released their juices. We attacked them with knives and forks.

We roasted red peppers until their skins blistered, steamed them in a covered bowl, scraped off their skins, and blended the pulpy flesh with cumin, chili powder, and oregano into a flamingo-pink sauce. We cooked mushrooms with garlic and onion, rolled the vegetables in steamed corn tortillas, and nestled them into a casserole dish. We covered these completely with the pink sauce, sprinkled the top with cheese, baked briefly, and served in squares topped with avocado slices and bright cilantro leaves.

It was December and we were waiting.

After urging Jonah to make a plan for college applications, after encouraging his expansive dreams of Colorado and Arizona, I did some research of my own and received a harsh reality check. I was shocked by the out-of-state-student price tag for Jonah's choices, and the more I thought about it the less I could see how we'd make it work. How could we even afford his plane tickets back and forth? It dawned on me that Jonah's unpreparedness for college was nothing compared to ours. With no savings, I didn't know how we were going to pull this off. I only knew that we would pull it off—that we had to, somehow.

My research brought me quickly to the University of Illinois. The price tag was still a shocker. I could remember when it cost just a few hundred dollars a semester to attend an in-state public university; now it was many thousands of dollars. But the price— for the quality and proximity—was tolerable. I knew Jonah could get a great education at the U of I. But first I had to shatter his dreams of heading west. Jonah has always been reasonable. When he was two years old and I was ready to wean him, I simply said, completely matter-of-fact, "I'm out of milk. It's gone." He nodded his head, a little sad, but with complete comprehension. He got it. I felt I could be similarly straightforward with him about college. "We need you to go in-state," I explained. What could he say? "Fine," he said, sighing.

Jonah and Jake drove to Champaign-Urbana for a visit and tour, and Jonah was notably cheerful afterwards, impressed by the size, diversity, and bustle, not to mention the all-you-can-eat food court. "Would you feel OK about going there?" I asked. "Yep," he said. "I think it'll be good."

I should have urged Jonah to apply to a few other in-state schools, and he should have taken it upon himself to do some research on his own for other options, but I didn't and he didn't, and that's how Jonah happened to fill out one and only one college application. So much for binders, so much for choices. But, I told him, you can go someplace more exciting for graduate school. Or go work wherever in the world you want to after graduation. You could study abroad for a semester.

He applied for an early decision, which meant he would hear something by mid-December. Back in the fall, when he'd applied, I'd had no doubt that he'd be accepted, but the weeks wore away my confidence. What if he didn't get in? What then?

By early December, I dwelled in a quiet, permanent state of freakedoutedness. I turned to food and pulled Jonah along with me. The cooking lessons changed tone. I lacked the focus and energy for pedagogy, and Jonah lost interest in taking notes. I simply grabbed him a couple times a week. "Come on," I said, "Tonight we are making fish in a pouch." It was sublimation, an effective distraction, a form of therapy, and had the added bonus of ensuring that we ate extremely well.

These were quieter lessons. Sometimes we barely talked at all. Sometimes my anxiety leaked out. "What if you don't get in?" I said once—only once—immediately regretting that this sentence had escaped. "Gap year?" said Jonah simply, cluelessly. I knew better than to react to that and turned my attention back to garlic and butter. Food was safe territory. Better to linger there.

My worry built to an absurd frenzy until the evening of December 12. The Day. It was five, already dark out, and I walked home from work through downtown Evanston, clutching my cellphone, waiting for Jonah to call. There were three possibilities: declined, accepted, or wait-listed. My phone finally rang. It was Jake, not Jonah. "Jonah has something to tell you," said Jake. I screamed, "Put him on!" and started walking faster.

"I got in, Mother," said Jonah. He sounded happier and more relieved than I'd imagined he would. I walked faster and faster toward home, almost running.

So many of my significant moments with Jonah have occurred at a distance, with me smashing my cellphone into my ear, practically running down a street, or pacing in a hallway, my heart pounding. Almost a year after the good news came about his acceptance to the U of I, and there we were again, talking on the phone. I was standing in front of a vending machine in Crowe Hall at Northwestern University, on a short break from the evening Spanish class I was taking. I had never mastered a foreign language, though I had studied a little French and Latin in high school, and later graduated from college with a degree that didn't require language proficiency. It bothered me. I felt like a stupid American. The class was a crushing challenge to my middle-aged brain. I liked the feeling of stretching myself, I loved the language, but I wished I'd started earlier. Like twenty-five years earlier.

I eyed a bag of peanuts through the vending machine glass and caught up briefly with Jonah. I could hear in his voice that he'd called for a reason, not just to chat.

"So," I said. "What's up?"

"Well," he said. "I've been thinking."

Uh-oh.

"I want to transfer to a different school. I am looking at Columbia College in Chicago." We talked, I did my best not to lose it, and my break ended. I sat in Spanish class, unable to pay attention, my middle-aged brain refusing to even try.

I wanted Jonah's life to be better than mine. I didn't want him to end up in his forties feeling like a loser for only being able to speak English, or whatever the equivalent would be for him. I was vehemently opposed to his idea to transfer. Jonah had been doing well at Illinois. He was in the Honors Program, was part of a living/learning community, and was taking a class in advertising that had piqued his interest. He was leaning toward declaring a major in advertising. It's hard to articulate how glad his new sense of direction had made me. His financial life wouldn't be the big mess that mine had become. Maybe his children would be able to go to college out-of-state if they wanted to. Maybe he'd learn Spanish, or some other language, in his twenties, rather than in his forties. I wanted Jonah to be successful, secure, happy. But "secure" and "successful" sounded like bullshit words, even to me, his mother, when I said them in my head. Jonah was orienting himself toward whatever complicated and interesting life he was going to have. My influence on him was waning.

So began my coming to terms with Jonah's change of plans. Columbia College is a vibrant art school in downtown Chicago. Jonah missed Chicago, he told me, and he admitted that he liked his classes at Illinois, but he didn't love the culture in

Champaign-Urbana, steeped as it was in Big Ten sports and fraternity life. Columbia offered a major in arts management, with an area of concentration in music business.

There was plenty of irony here for Jake and me. The music business! Hadn't it chewed us up and spit us out? Was Jonah's attraction to the music business connected, even subconsciously, to his parents' inability to manage the business side of our careers? Was this our family's equivalent to George W. Bush going to war in Iraq to succeed where his father had failed? The process of transferring was painful at first, but I visited the school and was impressed, and Columbia offered him a nice scholarship, which made it easier. Jonah remained resolute, and in the end it was the first great decision of Jonah's adult life. I'm glad he didn't listen to me.

I am glad that I didn't listen to my own parents when they advised me against moving from Indiana to Boston. I was eighteen. I could have stayed in Bloomington for a few more years and graduated from Indiana University (the only college to which I'd applied) as a twenty-year-old with a miniscule student loan debt and my options wide open. My mother didn't like the idea of my following my boyfriend out to Boston. He was going for a legitimate reason, to attend music school, while I was mainly just along for the ride, which struck her as overly dependent. In a rare moment of closeness, she told me about being engaged in her early twenties to a man she worked with in the civil rights movement. He was African American, and her family effectively disowned her. When her fiancé accepted a job in Chicago, she moved there to be with him. Most of her family, including her parents, brothers, aunts, uncles, cousins, lived in the Chicago area, but none of them would associate with the young couple. My mother accepted this. But in Chicago he broke things off.

"That was the worst winter of my life," she said. Cold, alone, and heartbroken, she set her sights on relocating to Tennessee, where she moved to work with the Southern Conference Educational Fund. That's where she met my father, who was working with the Southern Student Organizing Committee. When she called home to announce her engagement to him, her father said, "Well, as long as he's white."

She recognized her own mistakes in my moving to Boston. Of course, I wasn't risking expulsion from my family, but she felt that I was risking the loss of my own identity and the possibility of suffering heartbreak in a strange city.

My mother knew by then that I would do what I would do. She had scratched her head when I'd announced my intention to graduate from high school after my junior year. Already one of the youngest in my class, this had me walking out of there at the age of sixteen. My mom thought I should stay in high school and take more college preparatory classes, or another year of French or Latin, in order to really take advantage of my years of free education. Of course she was right, but I thought I was too cool for school. Being locked inside a big building all day made me feel like I was going to scream. I was restless and wanted the freedom of adulthood. My mother could have prevented me from actualizing this crazy plan, but I was grateful when she didn't. In fact, she wrote an excellent letter, petitioning on my behalf.

She also could have stopped me from moving out of the house immediately after I graduated. I found a room to rent in a house full of Indiana University sorority girls who thought it was funny to have a sixteen-year-old roommate. My mother advised me against it. "Stay home," she said. "Save your money." But she did not prevent me from moving.

And she knew that I would move to Boston if that was what I wanted to do. She was also distracted by a momentous event in her own life. My parents had, at this time, been divorced for thirteen years. My father remarried after a couple of years. My mother had a number of long-term relationships, but she had never remarried.

When I was eighteen, she and her friend Ahmet fell in love and decided to get married and move to his home country of Turkey, where he had a job offer and a daughter exactly my age. I was setting off on a big adventure to Boston; my mom was going on an even bigger one, permanently relocating to Turkey.

My father and I had a more comfortable and easy relationship, probably because I had spent less time with him (every other weekend and some longer stretches in the summer since I was five). But he was uncharacteristically stern and disapproving. "Let me be clear," he said. "I think it's a mistake. I think you should stay and complete your college education, not run off and start a band." He was right. Staying would have been the smart and responsible thing to do. But there was nothing smart or responsible about me at the time. My boyfriend was in Boston and I missed him. I was bored with Bloomington and craved adventure. I was hopelessly in love with music, and overcome with my romantic vision of starting a band with John. We would conquer the world. Never mind that I could barely hold onto a pair of drumsticks, never mind that I was lacking in ability and discipline. I had a dream. And all my parents' commonsense wisdom meant nothing to me.

It was my father who took me to the airport. My mother was in Turkey on a preliminary visit, meeting her new family. I can still see my father's face at the Indianapolis airport. Not angry. Worried. He gave me a little money, hugged me, and said goodbye, tears sitting in his eyes. I wonder what that moment felt like for him. Now that I'm a parent, I can kind of imagine. Later I learned that after I boarded the plane, he broke down and cried for the first time in his adult life. From the moment I boarded the plane, though, my parents were entirely supportive. Over the following years, as the Blake Babies began to garner some press attention, I clipped reviews and mailed them home. During a visit to Indiana one winter, I visited my father's office and found his walls entirely covered with every single clipping and photo I'd sent. My time in Boston was not easy, but those were exciting and fruitful years; I played music, met incredible people, tried a million different jobs, and stretched myself beyond my southern Indiana upbringing in ways that would enrich the rest of my life. It was a crazy decision. But it was one of the best crazy decisions of my life.

Jonah's decision to leave the U of I wasn't in this league of crazy. He was switching from one good college in Illinois to another, not exactly on par with my eighteen-year-old folly, or the drama of my mother's situation. Nobody was going to get disowned here. And really, should I have been surprised? Jonah had done what I'd wanted and wished for him to do all along. He had taken initiative, researched different programs, and found the right college for him. Better late than never. Everything fell into place, as it always seems to for Jonah, despite my worries.

I could have spared myself a lot of freakedoutedness if I'd just been able to relax into the uncertainty of my son's life, if I'd been able to trust him the way I'd blithely trusted myself at his age. I regret the needless stress I put myself through. But here's something I do not regret, something that has already, in my selective memory, begun to overshadow the difficulty of those chilly weeks of waiting: the comfort food that Jonah and I cooked to keep the home fires burning, those calm moments side-by-side in the kitchen making potatoes gratin with vegetarian sausage, fish in a pouch, stuffed portobello mushrooms, and mushroom enchiladas.

Potatoes au Gratin

For the potatoes, I use the slicing disk on my food processor, but slicing by hand is fine too. Just make sure the slices are very thin.

You can use smoked fish instead of vegetarian sausage, or regular sausage, or cubes of ham . . . or skip this entirely and go for a pure potatoes-and-cream experience!

Serves 4 generously

4 tablespoons unsalted butter

2¾ pounds russet potatoes, peeled and sliced ⅛ inch thick

Salt, to taste

Freshly ground black pepper, to taste

2 large cloves garlic, thinly sliced

1 14-ounce package vegetarian sausage, cut into big bite-sized chunks

3 cups half-and-half (amount might vary depending on depth of baking dish)

1. Preheat the oven to 350°F. Generously butter a 9 × 12-inch casserole dish or cast-iron gratin dish—use all 4 tablespoons of butter!

2. Cover the dish with a layer of potatoes. Cover with salt, pepper, ⅓ of the garlic, and ⅓ of the sausage pieces. Repeat this layering twice more, then finish with a last layer of potatoes, salt, and pepper on top.

3. Pour the half-and-half over the potatoes to just cover the top of the slices. Gently press down to submerge potatoes. Tightly cover with foil or a lid. Bake 1 hour, until the potatoes are very tender and knife goes through easily. This might take more than 1 hour; let it take however long it needs.

4. Increase the oven temperature to 425°F, remove the cover, and bake for 10 additional minutes to brown the top. Remove from the oven and let cool for 10 minutes. Slice and serve.

Fish in a Pouch

Adapted from a recipe in Emeril Lagasse's *There's a Chef in My Family!* I simplified the spice blend and added zucchini. For an easy and complete meal, make a pot of white basmati rice while the fish and zucchini cook.

Serves 4

4 tablespoons unsalted butter, softened

2 teaspoons Worcestershire sauce

2 medium cloves garlic, minced

1 teaspoon sweet smoked paprika

½ teaspoon ground white pepper

¼ teaspoon dried oregano

¼ teaspoon dried basil

¼ teaspoon dried thyme

⅛ teaspoon ground cayenne pepper, optional

1 teaspoon salt, divided

4 8-ounce white fish fillets, no thicker than ½ inch (any kind; tilapia and sole are great)

4 medium zucchinis, sliced into thin rounds

Finely minced fresh parsley, for garnish

1. Preheat the oven to 375°F.

2. In a small bowl, mash the butter together with the Worcestershire sauce, garlic, paprika, white pepper, oregano, basil, thyme, cayenne pepper (if using), and ½ teaspoon of the salt.

3. On each of 4 12 × 8-inch sheets of aluminum foil, place a fish fillet in the middle. Lightly season the fillets with the remaining salt and top each with 1 tablespoon of the seasoned butter. Evenly top with the zucchini slices.

RECIPE CONTINUES

4.   Fold each sheet of foil: Bring together the long edges of the foil and fold to form a tight seal. Bring the outer short edges in 1 at a time, and fold in twice to seal the sides. Bake the pouches, on a baking sheet, for 20 minutes.

5.   Serve immediately, a pouch on each plate—it's fun to let everybody open their own pouch, but be careful, the steam is intense! Sprinkle parsley on top before eating.

Stuffed Portobello Mushrooms

I make this for Thanksgiving every year for the inevitable vegan sitting at our table (for the past two years, this has been Jonah's college room-mate). It makes a good holiday main dish and goes well with the usual trimmings.

Serves 6

2½ cups vegetable broth, divided

½ cup brown rice, any kind, rinsed and drained

½ cup green or brown lentils, rinsed and drained

1 dried bay leaf

½ teaspoon sea salt plus a little extra for cooking onions

Big pinch freshly ground black pepper

2 tablespoons olive oil, plus more for brushing

1 medium yellow onion, chopped finely

1 cup raw cashews, chopped finely

4 cloves garlic, minced

¼ cup dried breadcrumbs

1 teaspoon dried basil

1 teaspoon dried thyme

½ teaspoon red pepper flakes

6 large portobello mushrooms, stems and gills removed

1. In a 2-quart saucepan with a lid over high heat, bring 2 cups of the vegetable broth to a boil. Add the rice, lentils, and bay leaf, and return to a boil. Reduce the heat to medium-low, cover, and simmer until the rice and lentils are tender, about 40 minutes. Remove from the heat and let sit, covered and undisturbed, for 10 minutes. Remove and discard bay leaf, then stir in the salt and pepper. Taste and adjust the seasoning as needed. Set aside.

RECIPE CONTINUES

2. In a large skillet, warm the olive oil over medium heat. Add the onion and a small pinch of sea salt and cook, stirring occasionally, 10 to 15 minutes, until sweet and golden. Add the cashews and stir a couple of minutes to lightly toast. Add the garlic and cook 1 minute more, stirring constantly. You don't want the garlic to brown.

3. Preheat the oven to 350°F.

4. Transfer the cooked rice and lentils to a large bowl. Add the onion mixture, breadcrumbs, basil, thyme, crushed red pepper, and the remaining ½ cup of vegetable broth. Taste and adjust the seasoning as needed.

5. Line a baking sheet with parchment paper. Place the mushroom caps on the prepared sheet and brush with olive oil to cover. Move them into 2 rows of 3, tops down. Divide the stuffing evenly between the mushrooms and bake for 30 minutes, or until the stuffing is nicely browned. Serve.

Mushroom Enchiladas with Roasted Red Pepper and Tomato Sauce

I hate when enchiladas are even slightly dry, so this recipe is very much on the saucy side. You can substitute roasted peppers from a jar if you don't have time to roast your own.

Serves 6–8

For the Sauce

2 large red bell peppers

2 tablespoons olive oil

1 medium onion, chopped

3 cloves garlic, minced

2 tablespoons chili powder

2 teaspoons ground cumin

1 teaspoon dried oregano

Big pinch ground cayenne pepper

Big pinch freshly ground black pepper

1 28-ounce can fire-roasted tomatoes

1 teaspoon salt

1 tablespoon fresh lemon juice

For the Filling

2 tablespoons olive oil

1 small onion, finely chopped

1 pound mushrooms, sliced

2 cloves garlic, minced

Salt and freshly ground black pepper, to taste

1 cup ricotta cheese

RECIPE CONTINUES

For Assembly

12 corn tortillas

2 tablespoons olive oil

1 cup shredded white cheddar or monterey jack cheese

Fresh cilantro leaves, for topping

Avocado slices, for topping (about ½ avocado per person)

To Make the Sauce

1. Preheat the oven to 500°F. Place the peppers on a baking sheet and bake for 30 to 40 minutes, turning 2 or 3 times, until the skins are charred and blistered. Remove from the oven and immediately transfer to a large bowl. Cover tightly with plastic wrap and let sit for 30 minutes. Reduce the oven temperature to 400°F.

2. Uncover the pepper and remove and discard the stems, seeds, and as much skin as you can. Coarsely chop the peppers and set aside.

3. In a deep skillet over medium heat, warm the olive oil. Add the onion and cook 5 to 6 minutes. Add the garlic, chili powder, cumin, oregano, cayenne pepper, and black pepper. Cook, stirring constantly, for 1 minute.

4. Add the tomatoes, chopped peppers, and salt and bring to a simmer. Reduce the heat to medium-low and cook for 15 minutes. Remove from the heat and let cool for a few minutes before carefully transferring to a blender. Add the lemon juice and blend until smooth. Taste and adjust the seasoning as needed. Set aside.

To Make the Filling

1. In a deep skillet over medium-low heat, warm the olive oil. Add the onion and cook for 10 minutes, stirring occasionally. Add the mushrooms and garlic and cook 8 additional minutes, stirring frequently. Add salt and pepper to taste. Remove from the heat, stir in the ricotta, and adjust the seasoning as needed. Set aside.

To Assemble

1.   Lightly oil a 9 × 13-inch casserole dish. Set aside.

2.   Warm a medium skillet over low heat.

3.   Meanwhile, using a pastry brush, lightly coat each tortilla with the olive oil.

4.   One at a time, warm the tortillas in the skillet, 3 to 5 seconds per side or until soft and warm; stack the warm tortillas on a plate as you work your way through them.

5.   Place about 2 tablespoons of mushroom mixture in the center of the top tortilla. Roll into a cylinder and place seam-side down in the prepared baking dish. Repeat until you have filled every tortilla.

6.   Pour the sauce over the top of the casserole dish. Sprinkle the shredded cheese evenly on top of the sauce. Bake until bubbling, 12 to 14 minutes. Let sit for a few minutes before serving topped with cilantro and avocado slices.

Soup is Good Food

J ONAH WAS A MERE FIVE MONTHS AWAY from his first year
of college. It was March, the nasty, dragged-out part of winter in Chicago, the perfect month for soup: lentil soup, hearkening
back to meals I'd enjoyed at the Hare Krishna temple in Boston;
black bean soup, a la Condo Pad, the apartment I shared with
John and Juliana, which was Blake Babies Central for awhile;
and New England Clam Chowder, a rich treat that also took me
back to my days in Boston. Jonah and I were in a steady groove of
weekly cooking lessons that felt like a fully integrated part of our
family life throughout this time.

Soup and money were on my mind that March. But money
most of all. Jonah's financial aid award letter arrived, and the

total amount that our family was expected to contribute made my heart stop. How did people do this? Tuition, housing, food, fees, books—it was overwhelming. Jonah was awarded a couple of small grants and a manageable student loan total, but the bulk of the bill would be paid out of our pockets. Our empty pockets. We could borrow ourselves and take out a low-interest educational loan. This was hard to swallow. I grew dizzy contemplating the already-massive pile of student-loan debt under which Jake and I were buried. Our payments were a monthly kick in the gut, scheduled to conclude when we were around 70, if all went well. How on earth could we possibly borrow more?

We could. We'd manage.

Managing makes me think of soup. And soup makes me think of Zirque, my younger brother. Once when I was on tour, I sent Zirque a postcard that had a homely photo of two bowls of soup sitting on a table. "Reminds me of you!" I wrote. That was probably twenty-five years ago, and soup still reminds me of my brother, especially as he was in the autumn of 1989, a freshman student of jazz performance at William Paterson College in New Jersey.

My brother has been a gifted upright bass player since high school. I always figured he'd go to music school, and I always pictured him in New York City. He'd landed very close. Again, I can't help but think of the stress we must have caused our parents, with one kid a music major in New Jersey, the other a college-dropout drummer in Boston. Did they envy their friends who had kids who were pre-med or majoring in engineering? Did they wish we were on more stable and potentially lucrative career paths? We were about as far away from stable and potentially lucrative as kids could be.

Zirque and I were not at all worried about the future. Maybe we should have been. We were enjoying our adventures. I hadn't seen much of my brother in the previous couple of years, and I was excited that he lived nearby. When the Blake Babies booked a gig in New York for that autumn, we arranged to stay with Zirque.

All was well in the world of the Blake Babies. We had made decent progress since that first thrown-together tour, and our period of disillusionment and bickering was still in the future. We had a smart, well-connected booking agent who represented bands like Sonic Youth, Yo La Tengo, and Big Dipper. We'd been "discovered" by Boston producer Gary Smith, who'd launched the careers of the Pixies and the Throwing Muses. Gary helped us sharpen our songs' arrangements in his stunning new recording studio, Fort Apache. Gary produced the songs on what became our first full-length release, *Earwig*. He helped us find a record deal, too, by introducing us to Jay Faires, who had just amassed substantial financial backing for his new record label, Mammoth Records, based in Chapel Hill, North Carolina. Gary and Jay had high hopes for the Blake Babies. At one preproduction rehearsal, Gary teased me about my dirty Jack Purcell sneakers. "I can't wait to see those at the Grammys," he said. We all felt a sense of momentum and promise. We had a long way to go, but things were moving in the right direction, we thought.

Nevertheless, we were dead broke. We made very little money playing shows, and didn't pocket a single cent from our record deal. During one recording session at Fort Apache, John, Juliana, and I ate Spartan packed lunches of leftover rice and plain cheese sandwiches while the engineer and producer used their per diems to buy expensive carryout Thai food. The smell of peanut sauce made me dizzy. At least somebody was getting fed off our record deal. We held jobs to survive. John and Juliana worked in record stores, and I was the assistant registrar at the Museum School in Boston. Around these jobs we juggled our increasingly busy Blake Babies schedule. We managed to cobble together enough money for rent and paid our bills with enough regularity to keep the lights on. We managed to buy drumsticks, guitar strings, and cigarettes. But we didn't have much money for food. We ate cheap pizza by the slice, onto which I'd pour a thick layer of red pepper flakes and Parmesan cheese. We made many home-cooked variations of rice and beans and stir-fry. And on those days when we couldn't even scrape together enough for those things, there was always the Hare Krishnas.

A few of the many broke musicians studying at Berklee had alerted us that free dinners were available at the Hare Krishna temple on Commonwealth Avenue. This vegetarian feast was open to everybody and only required that one speak politely to the rosy-cheeked devotees who circulated through the temple during mealtime with shining bald heads and flowing saffron robes, seeking converts. "Have you ever tried chanting?" they would ask, especially when they found out we were musicians. "*You* should understand the power of vibration," they insisted. Their aim was to persuade us to stay for the hours of chanting "Hare Krishna" afterwards. They promised that the chanting would change our lives, bring us everything we ever longed for. Today I wish we had done so at least once, just to see what it was like. But at the time we were only longing for their food, and we already had that. I loved the meals there: abundant, rich, everything swimming in ghee. I especially loved the rich, fragrant soup they always served. Today, any bowl of cumin-heavy dhal-like soup takes me right back to those dinners, to being a grubby musician in torn jeans on the floor of an incense-soaked, flower-filled temple in Boston's posh Back Bay.

We managed. Managing was part of the fun.

John, Juliana, and I drove down to Zirque's apartment in Paterson the day before our show in New York. No more touring in borrowed station wagons for us! We had gotten a used Chevy van, ours for just $1,000. We were now a three-piece, having returned Evan Dando to the Lemonheads and impending stardom. We

couldn't find an adequate replacement for Evan, so Juliana, un-
daunted, picked up the bass and mastered it instantly. We were
spare, pared-down, back on the road with only the essentials:
guitar, bass, drums, vocals, a cheap van with no crew, a box of
T-shirts to sell, and a bag of pistachios to eat (the shells spilling
out of the van when we opened the door). We never stayed in hotels if we could avoid it. We were, in a phrase we'd later hear from
the eternally quotable Mike Watt, "jamming econo."

It was certainly an econo move to crash at my brother's apartment. He was as broke as we were, but he was thrilled to put us up,
and had obviously cleaned his shabby place in anticipation of our
stay. He generously insisted on cooking dinner for the band. I was
impressed by Zirque's first attempt at living like a grown-up. He
paid rent and bills, maintained his own station wagon (a must for
lugging around his huge double bass), managed his time between
classes, lessons, and gigs, kept his kitchen stocked with practical
staples, and cooked himself dinner every night. All this at the age
of eighteen!

The summer before college, Zirque had scored a full-time
job in a café kitchen, and the owner had assigned him the task
of making the soup of the day. This was Zirque's crash course in
cooking basics, a rough equivalent to the cooking lessons I'd later
offer Jonah. He made around seventy pots of soup that summer,
mastering dozens of variations. By the end of the summer, Zirque
was very, very good at making soup.

He cooked us one of his specialties: split pea with squash. He
rinsed and drained a pound of green split peas, peeled potatoes,
chopped squash, crumbled in herbs. I was most impressed by the
squeeze of lemon juice he added at the end, "It wakes everything
up," he said. "Brightens the flavor." My kid brother! Zirque didn't
use a recipe—he never has and still never does. He claims that it
wasn't restaurant work that taught him the most about cooking,
it was jazz.

"Studying improvisation," he insists, "taught me to trust my-self, to taste, adjust, and keep the process alive." It was working.

Zirque exploited his soup-making skills in Paterson. He could make a pot of good food that was large enough to last several days and only cost him a few bucks, and he quickly gained a reputation in his seedy apartment building. Sometimes his roommate would foot the grocery bill in exchange for Zirque's doing the cooking. One day, the guys in the apartment downstairs knocked on his door: "We have broccoli, a can of beans, and some rice. Can you cook it for us?" His talent in the kitchen helped him to survive. Zirque, like the rest of us, was managing.

John, Juliana and I each ate a nice big bowl of Zirque's tasty soup. My brother had changed tremendously in the previous two years. He had spent his final year of high school at Interlochen Arts Academy in Michigan, playing music day and night, maturing into a real musician. Zirque told us about his classes in theory and performance, about his rigorous private lessons and his hours of daily practice. He was in love with it all. He dreamed of gigging in New York City, in the legendary clubs where his idols performed.

I was happy for Zirque and impressed by his passion, but I also felt shaken up by our conversation, humbled by his dedication and zeal. I mean, I was a musician too. We had that in common. But whereas I was happy to be part of a music scene, going out to shows and parties and feeling like I belonged, I lacked the focus and work ethic to really delve into my instrument. Since the Blake Babies had started, John and Juliana had improved dramatically as musicians; they were both in music school, taking lessons and practicing. I'd had occasional bursts of motivation when I would push myself to improve, but these were sporadic, and the impetus was difficult to muster. I liked being in a band, while my brother's connection to playing music was all encompassing. That other-wise happy night in New Jersey, my heart began to sink. I felt like an imposter. My brother was a real musician. John and Juliana were real musicians. I was a lucky hack.

I flopped around on Zirque's couch, not falling into the sleep I needed before the next day's gig, awash in insecurity and doubt. Should I even be doing this? Is this really what I'm meant to do with my life? If I could go back and have a few words with that twenty-year-old Freda, I'd tell her this: Get used to asking yourself these questions. And don't expect yourself to answer them definitively, ever. I found one ray of light on that painful night, something from the long talk we'd had with Zirque. He had described his process for preparing to perform. He warmed up extensively, running through scales and finger exercises in a focused, meditative state. He visualized playing the first note of the set, right in the pocket, totally present and powerful. As I finally drifted off to sleep, I thought OK, maybe I can try that in New York tomorrow.

In the morning, Zirque made us oatmeal and we drove into Manhattan's Lower East Side with my brother as our enthusiastic tour guide. This was his favorite neighborhood, and I could see why. The move from Bloomington to Boston had been a major leap for me, but New York made Boston seem tiny, dull, and mean. The Lower East Side in 1989 was edgy and vibrant. The buildings were mostly crumbly and derelict, almost bombed-out looking ("Welcome to West Beirut!" said Zirque), but the streets were alive, full of wild pierced women and beautiful leather-clad men.

Zirque took us to the Life Café, the very epitome of bohemia. I was dazzled. Each tabletop at Life was a collaged masterpiece. Sculpture grew out of the floor. Patrons played chess, ate cheap vegetarian chili, and read Kierkegaard. Jonathan Larson was probably sitting in there writing *Rent*. I ordered a soy cappuccino, mostly because I'd never heard of such a thing. It was the strangest, most exotic item I'd ever had a chance to order off a menu. It was delicious. My existential ennui and doubt from the previous night evaporated entirely. I was living the life, and it was a good life. The one I wanted to be living.

We loaded our gear into the Pyramid Club, a place as bohemian as the rest of the neighborhood. Vintage soft-core porn played silently on screens throughout the venue, and as I sat on the floor of the dressing room, hunched over my drum pad running through rudiments, gorgeous transvestites, there for the late show following our set, milled all around me, touching up their makeup in the brightly lit mirrors. I felt like a dude compared to them, down there on the floor in my jeans and sweatshirt, plain-faced. Plain, period. But I wasn't uncomfortable; I loved the Pyramid Club and I felt awake and alive. After a long warm-up my hands and brain felt awake and alive, too. Before we went on, I visualized the opening note to our first song, imagining myself strong and confident, not an imposter but a real rock drummer.

We had a good show at the Pyramid. Most gratifying to me was Zirque's enthusiastic feedback afterwards. "John's live sound is massive," he said, "but he manages to get out of the way of Juliana's little-girl voice." He rushed to add—"a little girl *who will kick you in the teeth*!" "And you and Juliana are a great rhythm section," he said. "Really idiosyncratic, nothing straight-ahead about it, but it's really, really good."

If only I could have brought Zirque along with me to all subsequent Blake Babies shows! My resolve and confidence would wax and wane in the years ahead, and more often than not, I'd find myself trapped in doubt. Zirque's passion for music and practice, and his philosophical approach to art and life, had steered me into a better place—but I just couldn't keep myself there. I could, however, steal his econo life-hack of making big pots of soup. Later, back in Boston, I would add black bean soup to our repertoire of Condo Pad staples, and it evolved into something not only cheap but truly delicious.

The Blake Babies stayed with Zirque a couple more times during his two and a half years in New Jersey. By the end of that time he was a junior in college and was gigging every Friday and Saturday night in Harlem with young jazz lions including Brad Mehldau, Joshua Redman, and Roy Hargrove. After the Harlem gig they would head over to the Blue Note in the Village for an after-hours jam. On the way there, they'd line up at Mamoun's for the best falafel sandwich in New York, which cost only $1.25. At each visit, I met a brother more accomplished and more at home in the city. I thought he'd spend the rest of his life in New York. But what I learned later was that he was exhausted. At 20 years old, he had been supporting himself for two years. He was struggling with his classes, always felt run-down, and was getting tired of being chronically broke. Soup, cheap falafel, and his intense love of music had sustained him through those years, but he'd run out of steam. Zirque dropped out of William Paterson and moved back to Indiana to regroup at our father's house. He had been too much on his own, with our mother out of the country and our father doing the best he could with limited financial resources. And his big sister, she was barely getting by herself.

Money anxiety aside, the month of soup lessons was steady and productive. Soup does everything I want food to do when I'm stressed out—it's warming, nourishing, and healing, it comes together with little fuss, and it goes down easy. Jonah seemed to have a knack for cooking and a growing appreciation for the process. Our soups were mostly cheap and simple, lentil and black bean, in keeping with our money situation at the time, although our clam chowder called upon some luxury ingredients that would have been inaccessible to me in my Blake Babies days. Baby clams were not in the budget back then. But that clam chowder was worth it. Yes, we were struggling, still paying off loans and worrying about Jonah's upcoming expenses, but we had jobs—we could afford the occasional can of baby clams! While Jonah and I stirred soup, I kept my mouth shut about our financial worries. He had an overall sense of the situation; I didn't need to drag him over the details. I was determined that Jonah would have every chance to succeed in college, that he wouldn't be distracted by making ends meet, that he wouldn't be too much on his own. I fervently hoped, though, that in the kitchen and elsewhere he would develop some of his uncle's discipline and determination, as well as his knack for improvisation. And I also hoped that he might develop some of his mother's knack for jamming econo.

Mung Bean Soup

Inspired by the dishes I loved at the Hare Krishna temple, this soup has evolved over the years to include kombu and miso, both ingredients I learned about in my macrobiotic days. I maintained the Krishna practice of excluding garlic and onions, foods considered too stimulating for serious spiritual practice. I think it works best in a pressure cooker, but the boiled version is good too.

You can find kombu at any health food store or Japanese grocery.

Serves 4–6

1 cup whole mung beans, rinsed and drained

6-inch piece kombu sea vegetable

2 tablespoons coconut oil or ghee

1½ teaspoons ground coriander

1 teaspoon ground cumin

½ teaspoon ground turmeric

¼ teaspoon freshly ground black pepper

2 tablespoons white miso

½ teaspoon salt

¼ cup chopped fresh parsley leaves

¼ cup chopped fresh cilantro leaves

1. In a pressure cooker, place the mung beans, kombu, and 6 cups of water. Cover, bring up to pressure, reduce the heat to low, and cook for 1 hour. Alternatively, boil in a heavy soup pot for 2 hours, replenishing the water periodically. The beans will almost entirely disintegrate in the cooking water.

2. Meanwhile, in a large skillet, warm the coconut oil or ghee over medium-high heat. Add the coriander, cumin, turmeric, and pepper and stir to lightly toast spices, about 30 seconds. Be careful not to let the spices burn. Remove from the heat and set aside.

RECIPE CONTINUES

3. After the beans have cooked 1 hour (or 2, if boiling), remove from the heat and carefully transfer to a blender. If there are large kombu pieces that have not dissolved, you can discard those. Small bits of kombu can just be blended in. Add the cooked oil and spices, the miso, and the salt and blend until smooth. Return the soup to the pot and gently simmer for a few minutes. Do not boil. Taste and adjust the seasoning as needed—this makes a fairly mild and delicately flavored soup, and you might want to kick it up a notch.

4. Serve hot, topped with the parsley and cilantro.

Zirque's Split Pea and Squash Soup

Serves 8, generously

10 cups vegetable broth, or water with a large vegetable stock cube added

1 pound bag green split peas, rinsed well and drained

2 dried bay leaves

4 tablespoons olive oil

1 medium onion, diced

4 stalks celery, including leaves, chopped

4 cloves garlic, minced

2 medium russet potatoes, peeled and cut into ½-inch cubes

1½ teaspoons dried thyme

Big pinch ground cayenne pepper

4 medium yellow summer squash, cut into ¾-inch cubes

Salt, to taste

Freshly ground black pepper, to taste

Fresh lemon juice, for serving

Minced fresh parsley, for serving

Sweet smoked paprika, for serving

1. In a large pot or Dutch oven, bring the broth to a boil. Add the peas and bay leaves; reduce the heat and simmer, uncovered, for 2 hours. Stir regularly—split peas tend to stick!

2. Meanwhile, in a large, deep skillet over medium heat, warm the olive oil. Add the onion and cook, stirring frequently, for 10 minutes. Add the celery and garlic and cook, stirring constantly, for 2 minutes. Add the potatoes and stir well to combine. Add the thyme and cayenne pepper and cook for 1 additional minute, being careful not to brown the garlic or burn the spices. Remove from the heat.

3. After the split peas have cooked for 1½ hours, add the vegetable mixture to soup pot.

RECIPE CONTINUES

4. After split peas have cooked for 1¾ hours, add the summer squash, salt, and pepper. Simmer for 15 additional minutes or so, or until all the vegetables are very tender. Taste and adjust the seasoning as needed. Remove from the heat and let sit for about 10 minutes before serving.

5. Ladle the soup into bowls, and top each serving with a fresh squeeze of lemon juice, a little minced parsley, and a sprinkle of sweet smoked paprika. Keeps well in the refrigerator for several days.

Condo Pad Black Bean Soup

Serves 3, doubles and halves well

2 tablespoons olive oil

1 small onion, thinly sliced

Scant ½ teaspoon plus pinch salt, divided

3 cloves garlic, sliced

¼ teaspoon allspice

Pinch ground cayenne pepper, or to taste

1 tablespoon soy sauce

2 15-ounce cans black beans, drained and rinsed

¼ teaspoon freshly ground black pepper

Fresh cilantro, to taste

Sour cream or Greek yogurt, to taste

1. In a medium pot over medium heat, warm the olive oil. Add the onion and stir until it sizzles. Add the small pinch of salt and reduce heat to medium-low. Cook, stirring occasionally, for 10 to 12 minutes. Add the garlic and continue to cook, stirring constantly, for 1 minute, or until the garlic sizzles but does not brown. Add the allspice and cayenne pepper and stir for 30 seconds. Add the soy sauce and stir well. Add the beans and 4 cups of water and bring to a boil. Reduce the heat back to medium-low and simmer, stirring occasionally, for 20 minutes.

2. Add the pepper and the ½ teaspoon of salt. Taste and adjust the seasoning as needed.

3. Using a regular or handheld blender, blend the soup until smooth. Serve topped with cilantro leaves and a big spoonful of sour cream or Greek yogurt.

New England Clam Chowder

My testers loved this recipe, especially the hot smoked paprika, the one-pot ease, and the quick cooking time.

Serves 4

2 tablespoons unsalted butter

1 medium onion, finely diced

2 stalks celery, quartered and thinly sliced

1 teaspoon plus pinch salt, divided

3 tablespoons all-purpose flour

2 10-ounce cans baby clams, in juice

1 pound (approximately 2 medium) Idaho potatoes, peeled and cut into ½-inch cubes

2 cups half-and-half

2 dried bay leaves

½ teaspoon freshly ground black pepper

½ teaspoon hot smoked paprika

4 tablespoons finely chopped fresh parsley

1. In a medium saucepan over medium-low heat, melt the butter. Add the onion and celery and a tiny pinch of salt and cook for 15 to 20 minutes, until very soft. Add the flour and cook, stirring well to combine and to lightly toast flour, 1 to 2 minutes.

2. Slowly whisk in 1½ cups of water until there are no lumps. Add the clam juice (don't add the clams yet!), potatoes, half-and-half, bay leaves, salt, pepper, and paprika. Increase the heat to medium-high and stir constantly until the mixture comes to a simmer.

3. Reduce the heat to medium-low and cook, covered, until the potatoes are fork-tender (15 to 20 minutes). Add the clams. Adjust the seasoning as needed. Remove and discard the bay leaves. Remove from the heat and let the chowder sit, covered, for 2 minutes before serving. Serve garnished generously with parsley.

CHAPTER EIGHT

Let Him Make Cake

IT WAS NOBODY'S BIRTHDAY, but Jonah and I were making birthday cake, a simple yellow layer cake with chocolate frosting. There was no chance of our skipping this cooking lesson. Cake had always been high on the list of foods I wanted to teach Jonah to make. Not because we ate cake all the time. We hardly ever did. It was the same when I was a kid. My mom baked on occasion, but sweets were not an everyday thing in her healthy hippie kitchen. Cake was rare and special, which is why I especially loved and anticipated our annual ritual of choosing my birthday cake.

Once a year, as The Day approached, my mother would ask, "What kind of cake do you want this year?" There was no wrong answer. I could have whatever I wanted. Some years I requested something exotic, like mint chocolate chip ice-cream cake from Baskin-Robbins or poppy seed cake with cream cheese frosting from Rudi's Bakery. Usually, though, I'd ask for the classic. "Regular," I'd say. Yellow with chocolate frosting, homemade.

Cake wasn't basic in the way of roast chicken or lentil soup. Cake was about more than survival and thrift. Cake stood for love, nurturing, indulgence, and celebration, and it was a key to my vision of a happy family, a healthy partnership. All that seems pretty normal, but for me, cake extended beyond this straightforward context. It had become tied to thornier issues of gender equality and to my identity as a woman and a feminist. And I'm not sure how normal this is. I wanted to convey to Jonah that this was important, that this cooking lesson had, um, layers to it.

A heavy agenda for that sunny spring afternoon. It was too much, really. To further intensify everything, I was coping badly with some intense motherly pangs. Jonah's high school graduation and eighteenth birthday were imminent. The year was whizzing by. I'd made a cake exactly like this one for his first birthday. It had resulted in the familiar classic image: chocolate frosting on a chubby little face. I'd made it again, with Jonah standing by my side on a chair, to celebrate his entering first grade. Was that the last time we'd made cake together? Twelve years earlier? And would this be the last time we would ever make cake together?

It's a good thing Jonah couldn't read my mind. Best to focus on butter and sugar. My background as a baker equipped me with some technique to impart. I showed Jonah the process of creaming these two ingredients together, whipping lots of air into the mixture, even if it takes longer than your arms want it to take.

"Skimp on this," I said, "and you'll end up with a flat, oily cake. You want it to be high and light."

Jonah jumped gamely in with a wooden spoon. Now he was occupied. Captive, you might say. Now I could regale him with my carefully chosen cake anecdotes.

First the one about my friend Jeannette, married to a man who shares all the domestic family work of cooking, laundry, and parenting. But on a recent night out with Jeannette, I'd asked her what she had planned for her upcoming birthday.

"Well," she said, "I'm going to make myself a chocolate cake."

I protested. "Shouldn't somebody be making a cake *for* you?"

"Yeah," she said, "but it's just easier if I make it myself."

"Seriously," I said to Jonah, while he vigorously beat the butter and sugar, switching hands when his arms fatigued. "I know too many women who make their own birthday cake."

"Hmm," he said.

"I mean," I said, willing to belabor the point, "is that sexist?"

"I don't know," said Jonah, thinking about it. His butter and sugar mixture was turning fluffy and lemon-colored, just the way it was supposed to. "Maybe it's not really sexist if men like to grill steak and women like to make cake. It covers more territory. Divides the labor." He paused. "Did her husband cook her dinner for her birthday?"

I didn't know. I tried to figure out how to explain that this kind of gendered division was problematic, that the whole "dad-makes-pancakes-and-barbecue-mom-makes-everything-else" tradition is not ideal. This arrangement lets Dad get applause for stepping into the kitchen every now and then for fun or novelty, while the everyday, unspectacular domestic responsibility remains squarely on Mom's shoulders. I wanted to raise boys who would become men who cooked for their families and friends without it being some kind of special event.

I instructed Jonah to mix in the eggs and vanilla and he resumed beating. He moved his face down into the bowl and inhaled vanilla.

"But too bad for men," said Jonah, "if they don't get to make cake."

"Or too bad for women," I said, "if they have to make their own birthday cake."

"Yeah," he said. "I get it."

I wanted him to get it. I know there are many birthday cake-making men out there, but I seem to have a lot of female friends who make their own, or who at least have to manage the process. One of them recently took it upon herself to print up a simple chocolate cupcake recipe and hand it to her husband. He took the hint. Jake and I, after more than twenty years together, have never solved the birthday-cake conundrum. Some years he buys one. Once or twice he's baked for me with a recipe I pointed him to. And I've certainly made my own. I honestly long for that annual ritual from my childhood. What I really wish is that Jake would ask me what kind of cake I want. I'd say, "regular." But, clearly, there is nothing regular about any of this business.

Jonah and I moved on to the dry ingredients. While he whisked, I launched into another cake anecdote, the one about my friend Paul. Paul and his girlfriend were on slightly shaky ground when he called me in a panic, the day before her birthday. He wanted to give her a cake, and his instinct was that it would mean more if he made it himself. Damn straight. His girlfriend was vegan and didn't eat refined sugar. "No problem," I said. Over the phone I dictated a shopping list, recipe, and detailed instructions for a vegan, naturally sweetened carrot and ginger cake. The next time I saw Paul's girlfriend, she hugged me.

"I was so surprised," she said. "I couldn't believe he made me a birthday cake."

"See," I said to Jonah, "sometimes cake matters a lot."

"Uh-huh," he said. As always, I had to trust that some of my sermon was sinking in. It was time to lay off my agenda and just enjoy the process. Jonah *did* seem to enjoy it. Maybe he'd grow up to be a man who made birthday cake. Maybe someday I'd receive a grateful hug from his partner. That seemed like a somewhat base motivation, but I knew there was a nobler one contained within it. Jonah and I chatted through the rest of the process, baked the cake, whipped up the frosting, and assembled it into tall layers with classic chocolate swirls. I'd kept Jonah in the kitchen a long time. He was antsy to go meet his friends.

"Shouldn't we have a piece?" I said.

"Save me one," he said.

So there I sat alone, eating the delicious cake my son made on his way out the door. The kitchen was a disaster, flour and powdered sugar everywhere. I still needed to teach Jonah how to clean up.

It sometimes bugged me that I was the primary cook in my family. The division of kitchen labor in my marriage was surprisingly traditional and gendered. In some ways it was simple: Jake didn't really know how to cook, and I did. He didn't particularly enjoy making food, and I have always loved to. Early in our relationship, we fell into a groove. There were times when things turned topsy-turvy and I shifted the cooking workload. In the weeks before Jonah was born, I created a hand-printed leaflet called *The Man's Cookbook*, comprising simple recipes for Jake to use during my postpartum recovery and babymoon, things like oatmeal, scrambled eggs, and stir-fry. *The Man's Cookbook* was a success and Jake used it heavily. Soon, though, I was back on my feet and we fell back into our usual groove. Many years later, I accepted a demanding full-time job as a leasing agent that required my working until seven or so. Jake was in graduate school and his schedule was relatively flexible, and we had two mouths to feed by this time. Jake was going to have to cook dinner. I made a new version of *The Man's Cookbook* with slightly more sophisticated recipes: Coconut Milk Curry, Vegetables Lo Mein, Fish in a Pouch. Again, success. Jake cooked up a storm. And throughout the years I left home to play shows, sometimes for two or more weeks at a time, and Jake did everything then, put every meal on the table, and didn't bat an eyelash. But always, when circumstances changed, we snapped automatically back into our regular groove.

Some people just aren't all that into cooking and it's not fair to be bothered by it. I dearly hope, though, that my sons will resemble me more than their father in the cooking department. Jake has always been willing to take on the task when necessary and has always done a fine job of it. That earns him points. He also is an excellent prep cook, glad to chop vegetables, freakishly skilled at floretting broccoli, and best of all he has always taken charge of dishwashing and kitchen cleaning. No matter what wreck I leave the kitchen in, I can count on an efficient and uncomplaining Jake to swoop in and deal with it. He would make fast work of my and Jonah's post-cake flour and powdered sugar disaster. I'd leave it to him.

One male member of my nuclear family needed absolutely no coaxing into the kitchen. Henry, thirteen years old, buzzed impatiently around the kitchen on a regular basis, wondering why he wasn't getting cooking lessons but insisting that he didn't even need cooking lessons. He could figure it out on his own. He just needed an opportunity. Henry had always had a rampant sweet tooth, and the birthday cake lesson inspired him to use his own money to buy a cupcake cookbook. He was confident, but I insisted on supervising him as he began to bake and frost batch after batch of mini-cupcakes. Jonah's birthday and graduation celebrations were approaching, and Henry asked if he could make cupcakes for both celebrations. I resisted. We'd planned a big party for graduation. All of Jonah's grandparents would be there, along with most of his uncles, aunts, and cousins. I wasn't sure if I could trust Henry with the responsibility for dessert. Henry insisted, so I gave him a test run—he could make cupcakes for Jonah's birthday, which would be a relaxed family affair with just the four of us.

Henry chose banana cupcakes for Jonah. He decorated them with chocolate frosting, spelling out "Happy Birthday Jonah," with one chocolate letter on each little cupcake. They were perfect: both cute and scrumptious.

"Henry," I said, "you are totally in charge of dessert for Jonah's graduation party."

Henry didn't look surprised. I mean, of course he was going to be in charge of dessert for Jonah's graduation party. He'd never doubted it for a moment.

The weather was sunny and mild on the day of Jonah's graduation. We survived the long, massive commencement ceremony and then met in the back garden of our apartment for a feast. This was a rare gathering. My mother had flown in from Turkey and my brother from Arizona. My father and stepmom drove up from Indianapolis, and Jake's parents, his sister and her husband, and their three kids (aka "the cousins") drove from Bloomington. Jonah requested a Mediterranean-style mezza, based on his fond memories of meals during a family vacation in Turkey, and my mother and I assembled a snazzy spread of tabbouleh, roasted eggplant, stuffed grape leaves, green salad, and spicy hummus. We bought cheese and olives and bread. Henry stole the show with his most elegant cupcakes yet: miniature chocolate cakes topped with whipped cream and a single raspberry. The cousins, it is reported, discussed them in awe on the drive home.

Perhaps my scattered efforts, from *The Man's Cookbook* to the Jonah cooking lessons, were paying off. Maybe these projects were having a trickle-down effect, inspiring Henry to move into the kitchen himself. Or was he, like me, just someone naturally inclined toward preparing food? I wasn't sure, but the kitchen was starting to feel less like my solitary domain and more like a space for everybody in the family. I was either doing something right, or something right was happening on its own. One thing is certain: My boys know how to make cake. And that is something that every boy should really know how to do.

Yellow Cake with Chocolate Frosting

Makes 1 cake

½ cup unsalted butter, room temperature, plus extra for greasing

1 cup plus 2 tablespoons granulated sugar

2 eggs plus 1 egg yolk

1½ teaspoons vanilla extract

2 cups all-purpose flour

1 tablespoon baking powder

1 teaspoon salt

1 cup whole milk, divided

Chocolate Frosting

⅔ cup unsweetened cocoa powder

½ cup unsalted butter, room temperature

3 cups powdered sugar, sifted, divided

⅓ cup milk or half-and-half, divided

1 teaspoon vanilla

1. Preheat the oven to 350°F. Grease two 8-inch cake pans with butter and set aside.

2. In a large bowl, beat the butter with a wooden spoon until very smooth. Add the sugar and beat vigorously until the mixture is light and fluffy. You can also do this in a stand mixer with the paddle attachment, or with a handheld mixer. Add eggs and egg yolk and stir well to combine. Add the vanilla and stir well. Set aside.

3. In a medium bowl, whisk together the flour, baking powder, and salt.

RECIPE CONTINUES

4. Add ⅓ of the dry ingredients to the butter mixture, along with ⅓ cup of the milk. Stir gently. Continue alternating ⅓ of the dry ingredients and ⅓ cup of the milk until all the ingredients are combined. Beat until the batter is smooth. Pour into the prepared pans and bake for 30 to 35 minutes, or until a toothpick inserted in the center comes out clean.

5. Let the cakes cool in the pans on wire racks for 10 minutes. Invert the cakes out of the pans onto the wire racks to cool completely before frosting.

6. While the cake cools, make the frosting. In the bowl of a stand mixer, or in a medium bowl with a handheld mixer or wooden spoon, beat the cocoa and butter together. Beat in 1 cup of the powdered sugar and ⅙ cup (8 teaspoons) of the milk or half-and-half. Beat until well combined. Repeat with remaining the powdered sugar and milk, add vanilla, and beat until creamy and smooth.

7. To frost, place 1 cake layer on a plate and spread a thick layer of frosting on top. Place the other cake layer on top, and frost the top and side. Serve immediately.

Vegan Banana Cupcakes with Vegan Cream Cheese Frosting

Makes approximately 36 mini cupcakes

1 cup mashed very, very ripe banana (2 large bananas should do the trick)

½ cup canola oil or melted and slightly cooled coconut oil

½ cup soy milk or coconut milk

1 tablespoon vanilla extract

1¾ cups all-purpose flour

1¼ cups granulated sugar

1 tablespoon baking powder

1 teaspoon cinnamon

½ teaspoon salt

Vegan Cream Cheese Frosting

1 8-ounce container cream cheese substitute

½ cup vegan margarine

2 cups confectioners' sugar, divided

1½ teaspoons lemon juice

1 teaspoon vanilla extract

1. Preheat the oven to 375°F. Line 36 mini-cupcake cups (3 12-cup pans should do the trick) with paper liners. Set aside.

2. In a medium bowl, combine the banana, oil, soy or coconut milk, and vanilla and whisk to blend well. Lumps of banana are fine. Set aside

3. In a large bowl, whisk together the flour, sugar, baking powder, cinnamon, and salt. Gently stir in the banana mixture, just until incorporated. Do not over-mix.

RECIPE CONTINUES

4.   Fill each prepared cupcake liner ¾ full and then bake for 9 to 10 minutes, until a toothpick inserted in the center of a mini-cupcake comes out clean. Let cool for 1 to 2 minutes in the pans before removing from the pans to let cool completely.

5.   While the cupcakes cook, make the frosting. In the bowl of a stand mixer fitted with the whisk attachment (or in a large bowl using a handheld mixer), beat the cream cheese substitute and vegan margarine until smooth. Add the powdered sugar, ½ cup at a time, until combined. Add the lemon juice and vanilla extract and beat until the frosting is fluffy and light. Frost the room-temperature cupcakes and serve.

Vegan Ginger–Carrot Cake with Maple–Orange Glaze

Makes one 9-inch cake

For the Cake

¾ cup apple or pear juice

½ cup melted and slightly cooled coconut oil, plus a little extra
    for greasing the pan

½ cup raisins

½ cup maple syrup or agave syrup

Zest of 1 orange (save the orange for the glaze!)

1½ cups grated carrots (3–4 carrots, depending on size)

2 cups all-purpose or whole-wheat pastry flour

2 teaspoons ground ginger

1 teaspoon baking powder

1 teaspoon baking soda

1 teaspoon ground cinnamon

½ teaspoon ground nutmeg

½ teaspoon salt

1 cup coarsely chopped walnuts, optional

For the Glaze

3 tablespoons maple syrup

2 tablespoons fresh orange juice

1. Preheat the oven to 350°F. Lightly oil a 9-inch round cake pan.
    Set aside.

2. In a blender, place the apple or pear juice, oil, raisins, syrup, and
    orange zest. Blend until smooth and emulsified. Add the carrots
    and pulse a couple of times to combine.

RECIPE CONTINUES

3. In a large bowl, whisk together the flour, ginger, baking powder, baking soda, cinnamon, nutmeg, and salt. Gently fold in the apple-juice mixture and stir in walnuts, if using.

4. Pour the batter into the prepared pan and bake for 40 to 45 minutes, until toothpick inserted in center comes out clean.

5. Meanwhile, make the glaze. In a small bowl, whisk together the ingredients. Set aside.

6. When the cake is done baking, let cool in the pan for 10 minutes, then invert onto a wire rack. Using a pasty brush, brush the glaze over the top and side of the cake.

7. Cool for at least 20 more minutes before serving. Keeps well in the refrigerator for a couple of days, and makes a really good breakfast!

Chocolate–Raspberry Cupcakes

Makes approximately 48 mini cupcakes

1½ cups all-purpose flour

1 cup blonde coconut sugar, ground to a fine powder in the blender, or granulated sugar

Scant ½ cup unsweetened cocoa powder

1 teaspoon baking soda

1 teaspoon salt

1 cup mild or medium-strength coffee, room temperature

½ cup coconut oil, melted and slightly cooled, or canola oil

1 tablespoon apple cider vinegar

1 teaspoon vanilla extract

1 recipe Coconut Whipped Cream (recipe follows), or dairy whipped cream

6–8 ounces fresh raspberries

1. Preheat oven to 350°F. Line between 40 and 48 mini-cupcake cups with paper liners.

2. In a large bowl, whisk together the flour, sugar, cocoa powder, baking soda, and salt until well combined.

3. In a medium bowl, whisk together the coffee, coconut or canola oil, vinegar, and vanilla until blended and emulsified. Pour the wet ingredients into the dry ingredients and stir gently, just until combined. A few lumps are fine.

4. Fill each prepared cupcake liner about ¾ full and bake for 13 to 15 minutes, until a toothpick inserted into the center of a cupcake comes out clean. Let the cupcakes cool in the pans for 1 to 2 minutes, then invert onto wire racks to let cool completely.

5. Top each cupcake with a swirl of coconut or real whipped cream and a single raspberry. Store unfrosted cupcakes in a tightly sealed container—they keep well for a few days.

RECIPE CONTINUES

Coconut Whipped Cream

A revelation. Don't feel sorry for vegans anymore. This stuff is even better than dairy whipped cream.

Makes enough to frost 48 mini cupcakes

2 14-ounce cans coconut milk

2–4 tablespoons blonde coconut sugar, ground to a fine powder in the blender, or sifted confectioners' sugar or agave or maple syrup

½ teaspoon vanilla extract

1.   Place the coconut milk in the refrigerator for at least 4 hours, until the solid cream has separated from the coconut water.

2.   Remove from the refrigerator, scoop out the cream, and place it in a large bowl. (You can also do this in the bowl of a stand mixer fitted with the whisk attachment.)

3.   Add 2 tablespoons of the sugar, or other sweetener, and vanilla and, using a whisk or handheld mixer, whip until light and fluffy. Taste and adjust sweetness as needed. Use immediately to frost cupcakes.

CHAPTER NINE

The Order of the Universe

THERE WAS A MOMENT near the end of Jonah's cooking lessons when life achieved a kind of equilibrium. Much was settled—Jonah was going to the University of Illinois in eight weeks, we had a handle on the amount of money we'd need to cough up, we'd filled out his health forms and housing paperwork, and we'd sailed through his eighteenth birthday and his graduation. The next big event would be the drop-off in Champaign. Jonah's life was in order. Mine, on the other hand, was a bit of a mess.

I'd been grinding away at my temporary job for a year by this time, and I'd just been offered the position permanently. I had to consider saying yes to that offer. I liked the department, had become friends with some of the faculty and graduate students, and had reached a reasonable level of competency after months of floundering. I'd get a significant pay increase with the permanent position, and it was nice to be wanted. But the job was killing me. I enjoyed almost nothing about the work. The financial and budgetary tasks were painful chores. I operated out of a busy, open office and had no privacy or personal space. I felt trapped and unfulfilled. Nothing that I'd done professionally in my life and really cared about—twenty years of drumming in bands, earning a master's degree in creative writing and publishing stories, teaching yoga, teaching writing, baking scones—had prepared me to be a good department administrator. Nothing about it felt like a step forward. It would be a big fat step sideways. But it was the only job offer I had, and my oldest kid was packing his trunk for college.

There had been periods of time in my life when I was happy and healthy but wasn't making enough money, like when I was drumming in a cover band and teaching yoga. Then, there were times when I was working a lot at a day job and pulling in a decent paycheck, but I didn't feel fulfilled. When I was enjoying some success as a musician on tour, I struggled with being away from my family. When I was mostly at home as a mom, I grew restless and missed playing music. I despaired of things ever feeling in balance. Did balance even exist?

Ignoring my voice of fear (or was it my voice of reason?), I turned down the administrator job and entered the job market in a frenzy. I hoped to find a teaching position, something that would put my graduate degree in writing to good use. I wrote a million query letters and I tried to stay calm. I had eight weeks to find something. Would I be able to land in that perfect place that had always eluded me?

It was during this time, right in the heart of my frantic job search, that we embarked upon our one-week raw foods experiment. This was Henry's idea, inspired by his Uncle Zirque. Zirque had stayed with us for a few days after Jonah's graduation before flying back to Arizona. Zirque's days of jamming at the Blue Note were now a quarter-century behind him. After leaving college in New Jersey, he had lived briefly back in Indiana, where he met and fell in love with a woman from Arizona. Before long, they had a baby and settled down in Sedona. Zirque finished college in Flagstaff and accepted a position teaching music at the Verde Valley School, a progressive boarding school in the stunning red rock desert.

He also did his best to establish a musical career in a remote desert town, and quickly became *the* bass player in Sedona. He worked with the Greek New Age artist Chris Spheeris and the eccentric guitar genius Stanley Jordan. Both artists gigged far and wide, taking Zirque not only to Phoenix and Los Angeles, but on trips to Portugal, Russia, and Cyprus. He also played at clubs and resorts in Sedona. He'd carved out a good life for himself, and I was, as always, in awe of his dedication and increasingly versatile musicianship. Our lives had changed in many ways since our soup days, but some things were the same. Zirque still practiced all the time, and I still wondered what the hell I was doing with my life.

After his many years in Arizona, Zirque had become a real Southwestern guy. Tan and healthy, he jogged up mountains every morning. He had a Vitamix and knew how to use it. He ate a mostly raw, scrupulously clean diet, featuring lots of green smoothies, kale salads, and sprouted nuts. True to form, he insisted on preparing meals for us during his stay. He made a quinoa salad with a creamy tahini dressing, a vegetable salad with avocado and hemp seeds, and—best of all—a big batch of raw chocolate. He set aside some of the raw chocolate to create what might be the most satisfying vegan dessert I've ever had: coconut ice cream scooped into balls, coated in chocolate, and frozen until the coating formed a crisp, perfect shell. We all swooned over that one.

Obviously, we loved having Zirque around. Henry, in particular, bonded with his uncle and was fascinated by his mega-healthy diet and his spiels about the benefits of live enzymes and chloro-phyll-rich meals. I was intrigued too. So when Henry suggested the raw foods week, I was right on board. Jake had zero interest in this endeavor, but he was heading out of town on a research trip. Jonah didn't have strong feelings either way. He was occupied with his friends, and since he was living on a different schedule than the rest of us, he'd only be minimally affected. Still, he was curious, and I had vague plans to offer Jonah a cooking lesson on how to put together a meal-worthy, sustaining salad. Further-more, it was July. Every Saturday I came home from the Evanston farmers market with tomatoes, peppers, berries, peaches, beets, lettuce, zucchini, chard, and more. If there was a proper season for building all our meals around fruits and vegetables, this was it.

My understanding of the concept of seasonal eating was based on my indoctrination into the philosophy and lifestyle of macrobiotics. I had lived and breathed macrobiotics during a six-month stint when I worked and studied at the Kushi Institute, a macrobiotic community and center in the Berkshire Mountains of Massachusetts. Once again, cooking with my kids was yanking me directly back to my past.

I'd fled to the Berkshires when I was twenty-four, after the first of several times I quit music. The band I was running away from was Antenna: A band formed hastily in the wake of the Blake Babies dissolution; a band named by a Ouija board; a band comprising me, my ex-boyfriend, and the guy I was falling in love with. What could go wrong?

I shouldn't have joined Antenna in the first place. At that crit-ical juncture, I'd been uncertain about my plans and pondered starting a new life in Athens or finally finishing college. While I pondered, John wrote some strong new songs and I helped him record demos. We played a few shows in the Midwest with a cou-ple of different bass players, and then we hit the jackpot with a young hotshot who had been playing with a high-energy mod band in Bloomington. Jake Smith bled all over his bass, sang like an angel, was easy on the eyes, and—to my surprise—he said yes when John asked him if he wanted to play with us. My crush on him quickly overshadowed my interest in Athens or college. I decided to stick around.

The band was originally called Sway, after our favorite Rolling Stones song, but a litigious letter from a band that claimed ownership of that band name sent us searching for a new one. Jake and John and I had taken up the recreational habit of getting high and consulting the Ouija board, and when we asked about a band name the spirits spelled out "Antenna." I liked the simplicity of that single word, and its connotations of receptivity. I also liked that we'd opened our arms to the random element and had received a pretty impressive reply. The Blake Babies had employed a similar strategy. When we needed a name, we approached poet Allen Ginsberg after a reading and asked him what we should call our band. Ginsberg quickly surveyed us and said, "Blake Babies." And that worked out well.

Being in Antenna felt loose and free during those early months, which made for a welcome change of pace from the Blake Babies' tight, precise pop songs. Antenna songs were less distinctive than Blake Babies songs, but they were more fun to play. I was a little more confident on the drums, reaping the benefits of our heavy touring schedule and the extended preproduction we'd done on John's new songs. At an early Antenna show in Chicago, the sound engineer told me, "The first time Blake Babies played here I couldn't believe what a bad drummer you were—me and my friends' jaws just dropped. But you're pretty good now."

I think it was meant to be a compliment, but I must admit, I ran to the Antenna van and cried after hearing it. Then I dried my tears and played a full-on rock show. He was right. I was "pretty good." And I had been pretty bad. But I could have used little punk-rock Freda to whisper in my ear at that moment that being able to "play" isn't everything.

One of the drum tracks on the first Antenna record turned out to be my favorite recording of myself. "Snakes" was the prettiest song John had ever written, emotional and melodic, with a slow, hi-hat-centered groove. It was a recording that might have pointed a way forward for me as a musician. Maybe Antenna would work out, I thought.

Or maybe it was simply the path of least resistance. Nothing was more familiar and habitual than playing music with John. We continued to work with the same record label as we had in the Blake Babies, and the same booking agency, and we played in the same bars, often with the same bands. It was OK, but I quickly began to pay the price for making a major life decision by default. Antenna was hard. I liked some of our first record, but overall it was scattered and inconsistent, the work of a band that ran into the studio too quickly. We hadn't quite found our identity. I still suffered doubts about my ability and my commitment and wondered if there might be something else out there that I could do well and feel less conflicted about. And it was not a piece of cake to work with John and Jake. We weren't Fleetwood Mac, but there was tension. John and I had survived the rough transition into friendship, but a clean break might have been healthier than the path we'd chosen—being two-thirds of a three-piece band, touring in a small van, while I fell in love with our cute bass player.

Not only was Antenna hard, but we were also living hard, often drinking and smoking heavily into the night, sleeping long into the day, and eating terrible food. I'd strayed far from my strident and healthy Blake Babies days when I was likely to go running every day, when my drug of choice was fat-free frozen yogurt and my morning pick-me-up ginseng tea. As the Blake Babies had disintegrated, my health did too, gradually, as I fell off the wagon and back into some bad old habits. By the time Antenna was rolling,

I was in terrible shape both physically and emotionally. This, I think, is what finally pushed me out of the band. I wanted to clean up my act. I also hoped maybe I could find a new path in life, one that felt truly my own.

I was sad to go, and John and Jake were sad to lose me as a drummer. We were also all a little relieved.

Just like I'd turn down the administrative position at Northwestern without an alternate plan in place, I left Antenna without a clue. What would I do? I focused my search on yoga ashrams, health resorts, various centers of wellness and weirdness—after all, better health was my primary goal. As it turned out, I landed in the very epicenter of wellness and weirdness. The Kushi Insititute. It must have seemed abrupt and random to my friends and family, but I'd been aware of the place for a long time and had filed it in the back of my mind, where it had waited for years.

My friend Becca in Boston introduced me to macrobiotics. She'd given me a copy of *Zen Macrobiotics,* a quirky and compelling little book by George Ohsawa, the father of modern macrobiotics, and she'd cooked me some homemade macro meals, simple bowls of brown rice and vegetables. Becca hoped to study at the Kushi Institute herself and had told me about their work-study program, which came with room, board, and free classes in cooking, lifestyle, and philosophy. One could encounter macrobiotics all over the place in Boston, which was the original home of the Kushi Institute before its move to the Berkshires, and the macro community had maintained a strong presence in the city. I often shopped at Erewhon Natural Foods (Juliana had worked there for a spell), which was owned and largely staffed by members of the community. I was attracted to the thin, calm, sober people who walked the aisles of Erewhon, and I was intensely curious about the food—seaweed, millet, umeboshi plums, brown rice, miso. I became a fan of a local catering company that provided take-out macro meals to the Museum School Boston, one of my favorite places for lunch. Those meals made me feel amazing. They gave me a kind of clean, clear energy that I noticed and appreciated all the more because I wasn't drinking or taking drugs at the time. I also, unlike many of my friends, thought they were incredibly delicious. I could sense that this nutrient-dense food supported my choice to be sober and physically active. The food was plain: a scoop of brown rice or other whole grain, a pile of lightly steamed greens, a protein-rich helping of beans, tofu, or tempeh, a longer-cooked sweet vegetable like roasted squash, and a salty tangle of seaweed, hijiki or arame. When I ate this way, I grasped Ohsawa's promise of a better, happier, healthier life through eating grains and vegetables, chewing each bite a hundred times and working hard every day. This stuff resonated with me, and although I didn't embrace it entirely at the time, I thought that someday I'd want to delve more deeply into macrobiotics.

So it wasn't completely out of the blue when, post-Antenna, I called the Kushi Institute and asked about work-study jobs. I filled out my application, nailed the phone interview, accepted an offer, and boarded a Greyhound bus for Massachusetts. On the two-day bus trip, I realized that I had absolutely no idea what lay ahead. I'd done nothing to prepare myself physically, nothing to transition out of my terrible lifestyle. When I arrived in beautiful little Becket, I had a blinding headache from caffeine withdrawal, an itching discomfort from nicotine cravings, and a strong thirst for a strong drink. I felt gross and toxic and not at all certain that I hadn't made a major mistake.

It helped that I loved it there right away. I was relieved to have left the rock world far behind. I was in macro world now. The KI felt like part school, part retreat, part ashram, part commune, and part freaky summer camp. It was housed in a slightly run-down former monastery in the mountains and surrounded by extensive gardens. It was an easy place to love. Residential programs ran almost continuously, mostly one-week intensives for those hoping that the macrobiotic diet would heal them in some way. There were lots of sick people coming through the center, mostly people with cancer, accompanied by their shell-shocked but supportive partners. The week included lectures, cooking lessons, lifestyle suggestions, a yoga-like system of exercise called Do-In, and three amazing, nourishing meals a day.

All this programming required a lot of staff: teachers and cooks, farmers and food-production experts, marketing professionals and administrators, housekeepers and landscapers. The staff was a fascinating cohort of people, hailing from Germany, Italy, England, Japan, Canada, Mexico, and from all across the United States and ranging in age from nineteen to eighty-five, including high school dropouts and doctors. I'd never been around such a diverse group. They were into healing and they were into meditation, but they were not a bunch of starry-eyed hippies. They were tough and funny and smart and all misfits in various ways. Just like me. And very, very into food. Just like me.

I worked in the main office from 9:00 to 5:00, answering the phone, greeting visitors, scheduling private consultations, and performing various clerical tasks. It was light work and left me with plenty of energy for other pursuits. Before work I went to Do-In class, meditated on my own or with a small group, or hiked into the Berkshires. One morning I had a close and thrilling encounter with an enormous black bear. After work I sat in on cooking classes or lectures, volunteered in the kitchen, or read in my room. After dark, when everybody except me was asleep, I sometimes tiptoed into the food-processing rooms to sneak a sample of delicious amazake, a sweet fermented rice drink, or into the kitchens to see if any good food was left from the day. I was often alone. My experience there felt like the exact opposite of being in a band.

When my fellow staff members at the KI found out about my background in rock, they usually asked if I missed playing music.

The honest answer was no. It felt nice to have slipped entirely out of that life for a while. Meanwhile, some of my musical pals were becoming full-on rock stars. One day I walked past a magazine rack in nearby Northampton to see Juliana looking stunning on the cover of *Sassy* magazine. Jake mailed me a copy of the Lemonheads' new album *It's a Shame About Ray*, and after one listen I realized that my old friend Evan—with some impressive help from Juliana—had produced a truly great record, one that would help to define a genre and a generation. I was amazed. And I was so far out of the game at that moment that I could only marvel. Maybe it would have been tougher for me had I been slogging it out in the business myself, but being at the Kushi Institute provided a comfortable distance from which to applaud the success of my former bandmates.

Gradually, I began to understand better what macrobiotics was all about. The macrobiotic diet is based on the principle that everything in the universe manifests into evolving forces of expansion (yin) and contraction (yang). This relates to food in that some foods are considered extreme, contracting, or yang, like meat and salt. Other foods are expansive, or yin, like fruit juice and sugar. For balance and good health, we should favor foods that reside in the middle of the continuum, which are mostly whole grains and vegetables. Foods that are locally grown and in-season are considered better suited for good health, and macrobiotics is critical of the modern supermarket, where produce shipped from all over the globe is available year round, regardless of season. Nothing is strictly forbidden in macrobiotics. Instead, the goal is balance, in the belief that too much extreme food throws the body out of whack and ultimately leads to illness. Whole foods, mostly plant-based, bring the body into harmony and health. There's a whole expanded philosophy behind it all, but this is the basic gist. Macrobiotics is about healthy living and harmonizing with the natural order of the universe. Pretty much the opposite of my experience with Antenna.

I definitely noticed both immediate and gradual changes in my health at the KI. The terrible headaches and insistent cravings went away. I started feeling great in response to the fresh mountain air, deep sleep, and amazing food. God, the food. I still dream about it. The rice was freshly hulled every day and the vegetables grown on site, all organic and of the highest quality. The tofu, tempeh, and miso were all made by hand and were all by far the best I'd ever tasted. And everything was prepared using local spring water by some of the most gifted cooks in the world. It might not have been the best food to everybody, but it was to me. It was exactly the kind of food I needed at the time.

I came to understand some of the fantastic claims for the healing benefits of macrobiotics. I had some strange physical transformations during those months. I'd had asthma since I was a child, and it briefly intensified in my early weeks at the KI—and then went away. Forever. I stopped menstruating for four months, but when my cycles resumed they were lighter and steadier, and recurring problems I'd had with cervical cysts vanished. Again, forever. My moods were up and down. Sometimes I'd feel elated, almost euphoric. Other times I sank so low I could barely deal with people. But that, too, evened out after a few months.

By the time I boarded a Greyhound bus headed back to Indiana six months later, I was detoxified and zealous, with a pressure cooker under one arm and a pickle press under the other. Booze, drugs, and cigarettes were far behind me, part of an entirely different life, I thought. I had fallen in love with clean living.

But I still had no idea what to do with my life. I'd wondered, when I'd first set off for the KI, if my fledgling relationship with Jake would survive our diverging paths and the long absence. During those months we talked on the phone often. I reported details of my strange days and nights, my tales of bears and amazake. He filled me in on the trials of recording the new Antenna record and his adventures on the road with John. He was contributing more songs to the band and had particularly enjoyed a stint of opening for Dave Lowery's band Cracker. Our connection only strengthened. I sent him a copy of *Zen Macrobiotics*, wondering what he'd make of all this "order of the universe" stuff, and I was delighted when he told me, soon after reading the book, that he'd been eating miso soup and brown rice. Jake was curious, open-minded, and respectful of my interests. This thing was looking promising.

A week before I took my return trip on the Greyhound, Jake called to tell me that Antenna's new drummer wasn't working out. Would I consider rejoining? I wasn't sure. But it was nice to be wanted. I'd hoped that running away would somehow lead me to a new path. Although it had been a great experience, I realized that my time at the Kushi Institute had been more of a time-out than a leap forward.

In no time at all I picked up the drumsticks again. The second Antenna record, *Hideout*, was coming out with good backing from the label, including a video budget and tour support. *Hideout* had strong songs, songs that I really liked, and things were getting solid with Jake and easier with John. I couldn't think of any good reason not to come back. I suspected that if I turned the offer down, I'd regret missing out. So I said yes.

And in only a matter of months I was thinking, *what have I done?* In the middle of a nine-week Antenna tour, a painful and unlikely pairing with the 1970s nostalgia band Jellyfish, I wondered how on earth I was going to quit the band, again, without seriously pissing everybody off. The biggest show on that tour was in L.A. Jellyfish had been all abuzz because Harry Nilsson was in the audience. That guy from the Black Crowes was there. I couldn't imagine anything less exciting; at the time, amazake seemed like way more fun. There was one really great moment for me that night, though, when I looked out into the audience and saw our old friend Evan Dando enter the back of the room and move through the club, an indie rock Moses parting the sea of the crowd. He turned every head. That was entertaining. But mainly everything was grating on that tour. I'd taken to complaining about things by saying, "That's so *yang*." I was turning orange from all the carrot juice I drank. I was totally not rock. I'd made a mistake. I wanted to be home doing yoga and making miso soup. I wasn't certain if I wanted to be playing drums at all, but I was sure that even if I did, Antenna wasn't the right band for me. I honestly liked the music, but it was too loud and aggressive, out of synch with my macro, mellow self. I felt terrible.

I shouldn't have worried so much. The universe soon interceded on my behalf in the form of a pregnancy test. Jonah was on his way, and I thought I was leaving music forever this time. Jake and I spent a few idyllic months as a little macro family with Jonah. We reenrolled in college and played house with our baby and then formed the Mysteries of Life, a quiet and laid-back answer to the loud rock shows we were weary of. We consciously created the band against the grain of almost everything we'd done before. After years of being urged by sound engineers to hit my drums harder, I began playing more with brushes and mallets and hit exactly how I wanted to, which was pretty soft. After bashing on cymbals in Antenna, I removed them from my kit completely. Jake abandoned all of his effects pedals and sang quietly in a natural, conversational voice, so as not to awaken Jonah. He wrote songs about being married and happy. We enlisted a cello player to round out the band. We gave up all attempts to be cool and successful. We just wanted to like what we were doing, and we wanted it to be on our terms. Who would have ever guessed that this band would be offered a record contract? It was such a surprise, we simply could not refuse. So there we were, baby in tow, deeper in the music biz than ever we'd been, and forced to redefine our notions of balance every day.

Henry and I jumped right into our one-week raw-foods experiment. According to the principles of macrobiotics, a raw foods diet is extremely expansive and yin, a diet that might be suitable during the warmest months of the year, or in a tropical climate, but one that would be weakening in the wintertime. Macrobiotics also argues that cooking food was a dramatic evolutionary leap for humankind, and that to reject cooking is to reject the distinct opportunity it represents to transform our food and improve our health. Thus, the dietary approaches of raw and macro are mainly at odds. However, both are considered healing diets and share certain characteristics: a strong emphasis on green vegetables; the avoidance of refined, processed foods; and a preference for organic produce.

I immediately felt energized on our raw diet. Maybe I needed a bit of expansion in my life. We ate smoothies for breakfast, lavish salads for lunch, and something that basically resembled salad for dinner. Jonah mostly fed himself on late-night sandwiches, but I corralled him and Henry into the kitchen for a quick how-to-make-a-salad-a-meal lesson. First of all, include a good source of protein, like nuts or hemp seeds. Secondly, embrace variety, including different colors and textures. Finally, indulge yourself; include a treat that you really love, so you won't feel deprived, like an avocado, a rich dressing, or some marinated mushrooms. That was it. Lesson over.

"All we eat is salad," complained Henry on day three. I tried to mix it up. I made a faux-pasta thing out of grated zucchini ribbons with a macadamia nut sauce. I loved it.

"This," said Henry, "is salad pretending to be something else."

We made it through the week. It helped that we made a big batch of raw chocolate using Zirque's technique. I took Henry out to lunch on our first day back to regular eating. He ordered a big portobello mushroom sandwich with a side of sweet potato fries. He poured a huge pile of ketchup on his plate.

I'd left my strictly macro days behind, although vestiges of those days survive in the way I cook and live, and I've never abandoned the quest for balance. I've just accepted that the quest is the point; the perfect state does not exist. The order of the universe is constantly changing, and it takes sensitivity and adaptability to navigate the fluctuations. And most of us mess it up most of the time. I do, anyway. I ran to macrobiotics because my life had teetered far out of balance. But I might have expected too much from brown rice. It gave me my health when I needed it. But it couldn't answer all of my questions and it couldn't make me perfect. But maybe it helped me embrace a broader view of perfection.

I watched Henry devour his ketchup-drenched fries. It was the exact right meal for a thirteen-year-old boy who'd been eating mostly smoothies and salads for a week. In fact, it was the very picture of perfection.

Finally, did the universe intervene in my job market woes? Well, yes. I believe it did so in the form of a bowl of candy. I'd added a candy dish to my desk in the department where I was temping in an attempt to cheer things up and make friends. It was like magic; people popped in for Jolly Ranchers and they lingered for conversation. One faculty member became a regular partaker and we developed a friendly rapport. One day, he came in for candy but also with a hot tip—the School of Communication was hiring academic advisors. "It's a faculty position," he said. "You mostly advise undergrads but you also get to teach. I think you'd be perfect for it."

Two months later, I moved into my new office.

Hijiki with Tempeh

I loved how much we all talked about food at the Kushi Institute, and certain foods were especially hot topics. Hijiki was one; people were obsessed with it, attributing it with all kinds of near-mystical beautifying properties, especially for the hair. Many of us found it to be an acquired taste. One woman told the story of how when she first became macrobiotic, she picked up pre-made macro meals for herself from a health-food store and brought them home to eat. "I hated the hijiki," she said, "so I fed it to my dog." But when she noticed that the dog's hair was starting to look amazingly glossy and thick, she started eating the hijiki herself. You can find hijiki in Asian grocery stores and natural food stores.

Serves 4–6

1 package dried hijiki seaweed (will vary in size from 1.76 ounces to 2.2 ounces, anywhere in that range is perfectly fine)

4 tablespoons canola oil or coconut oil, divided

2 tablespoons soy sauce

1 tablespoon mirin

1 package (8 ounces) tempeh, any type, cut into ½-inch cubes

2 carrots, julienned

4 tablespoons minced fresh parsley

1. In a large bowl, place the hijiki and enough water to cover. Let soak for 10 minutes, then drain and rinse in a colander. Set aside.

2. In a large, deep skillet over medium heat, warm 1 tablespoon of the oil over and add the hijiki. Stir to coat with the oil. Add enough water to cover hijiki halfway, increase the heat to high, and bring to a boil. Reduce the heat back to a medium simmer, add the soy sauce and mirin, cover, and cook for 25 minutes while you prepare the tempeh.

3. In a separate, medium skillet over medium heat, warm the remaining 3 tablespoons of the oil. Add the tempeh cubes and brown for 10 to 15 minutes, turning frequently. You don't have to brown every single side of every single cube, just do your best. Remove from the heat and drain on a plate lined with paper towels.

4. After the hijiki has cooked for 25 minutes, add the tempeh cubes and carrots. Check the water level and add a little more if it's getting dry. You want to keep the hijiki halfway covered. Cover and simmer for 10 more minutes.

5. Uncover and stir gently to combine the hijiki, carrots, and tempeh. Taste and adjust the seasoning as needed. If liquid remains, increase the heat to high to cook it off. Serve hot, garnished with parsley.

Strawberry–Banana Smoothie

When we were eating only raw food for a week, we usually had a smoothie for breakfast, and this is the version we eventually settled on as the ultimate. With multiple fruit and veggie servings and a dose of high-quality protein (and chocolate!), this makes a nourishing and energizing breakfast.

Serves 2

1½ cups strawberries (I like frozen for a milkshake-like texture)

1 banana (frozen if possible, but I always forget and it's fine)

½ cup micro-greens, sprouts, or baby kale

2–3 tablespoons raw cacao powder or unsweetened cocoa powder (not as delicious but still good)

2 heaping tablespoons hemp seeds

1½ cups nondairy beverage (almond, soy, or, my favorite, coconut)

1. In a blender, combine the ingredients and blend until smooth. Drink immediately.

Raw Slaw with Creamy Pine Nut Dressing

I ate this for lunch during our raw foods week and I loved it—the rich dressing provides enough fat and protein to make it filling and sustaining, and you can't help but feel good after consuming this quantity and variety of vegetables. One tester added minced cucumber to even further increase the amount of veggies. She also substituted sunflower seeds for the pine nuts and reported excellent results.

A food processor makes the vegetable prep a million times easier and gives a nice slaw-like texture.

Serves 4 generously

1 small bunch kale, stems removed, very thinly sliced (about 1 cup)
1 small red cabbage, grated (about 2 heaping cups)
1 small green cabbage, grated (about 2 heaping cups)
2 carrots, grated (about ½ cup)
1 recipe Creamy Pine Nut Dressing (recipe follows)

1. In a large bowl, combine the vegetables together well. Add the dressing, stir well, and taste to adjust the seasoning as needed. Chill for at least 30 minutes before serving.

Creamy Pine Nut Dressing

1 cup pine nuts
⅓ cup fresh lemon juice (about 3 lemons)
⅓ cup olive oil
1 tablespoon honey or agave
1 teaspoon sea salt

1. In a blender, place all the ingredients and blend until smooth and creamy. Add a little water, 1 tablespoon at a time, if necessary to thin it out. The dressing should still be on the thick side, like mayonnaise. Use immediately.

Peanut Butter and Miso Ramen Soup

I was making miso soup one day and wanted something richer and more filling—I added peanut butter, and it was a hit. I'd like to dedicate this recipe to an acquaintance of Jake's in the UK, who, when Jake told him about the popular American snack of peanut butter on celery, asked in disgust, "Is there anything you Americans won't mix with peanut butter?" This soup answers his question. Kombu, wakame, and miso can all be found in Asian grocery stores and natural food stores.

Try a combination of white and red miso; using two different types of miso gives a full-bodied flavor.

Serves 4

1 6-inch piece dried kombu

8 dried shiitake mushrooms

1 onion, halved

2 tablespoons soy sauce

2 tablespoons mirin

3 scallions, thinly sliced, divided

1 6-inch piece dried wakame

4 tablespoons miso

3 tablespoons creamy, unsweetened peanut butter

2 carrots, peeled and thinly sliced

3–4 cups tender, quick-cooking greens like baby spinach, baby kale, or watercress, or any combination

5–6 ounces ramen noodles or soba or udon noodles

1 pound extra-firm tofu, cut into ½-inch cubes

Hot pepper sesame oil, for topping

1. In a large pot, combine the kombu, mushrooms, onion, soy sauce, mirin, and ½ of the scallions. Add 8 cups of water and bring to a boil. Reduce the heat to a simmer and let cook, uncovered, for 25 minutes.

2. Meanwhile, in a small bowl, soak the wakame in water to cover for 5 minutes or so. Drain, chop into small pieces, and set aside.

3. In a separate small bowl, combine the miso and peanut butter. Scoop out some of the simmering hot broth, just a little, and add to miso. Mash and stir well with a fork to blend into a smooth paste.

4. After the broth has simmered for 25 minutes, strain the vegetables and discard all except the shiitake mushrooms. Return the broth to the pot and bring back to a gentle simmer. Stem and thinly slice the shiitakes.

5. Add the wakame, shiitakes, carrots, greens, and ramen noodles to the simmering broth. Cook for 5 minutes. Add the miso and peanut butter, the remaining ½ of the scallions, and the tofu. Continue to simmer (do not boil the miso—reduce the heat if you need to) for 5 minutes.

6. Serve hot, topped generously with hot pepper sesame oil.

Zirque's Vegan Chocolate Ice-Cream Balls

Serves 4

½ cup coconut oil

¼ cup coconut sugar

½ cup raw cacao powder, plus more as needed

1 teaspoon vanilla extract

½ teaspoon salt

1 pint mint chocolate chip frozen nondairy coconut dessert,
    such as Coconut Bliss

1. In a medium saucepan over low heat, melt the coconut oil. Add
    the coconut sugar and whisk well for a few minutes to dissolve.
    Whisk in the raw cacao powder, vanilla, and salt and stir for 10
    minutes or so, until the mixture attains a consistency thicker
    than syrup, but not as thick as frosting. Add more cacao powder
    if you need to. Remove from the heat.

2. Using an ice cream scoop, divide the coconut dessert into 4
    balls (they don't have to be perfect) in 4 separate serving bowls.
    Pour the cacao mixture over balls, dividing evenly to coat. This
    doesn't have to be perfect either, just try to mostly cover. It's
    also perfectly fine for some sauce to pool in the bottom of each
    bowl. It's all good.

3. Place the bowls in the freezer for 20 minutes (can be frozen for
    longer). Serve with spoons.

CHAPTER TEN

Popeye Pesto

JONAH WAS GONE and loaves of bread molded in the kitchen, apples softened and rotted, lettuce wilted, cheese dried up. For thirteen years we'd been feeding two boys, and for the past few years, hungry Jonah had consumed at least half the food in the house. After a while, we learned to buy less.

Jonah's first weeks at the University of Illinois were emotional for me, but I had a welcome distraction in my new academic advising job. That fall, I'd been assigned the entire class of incoming first-year students—Jonah's exact contemporaries! I'd lost one eighteen-year-old and gained seventy-six. I spent hours in my office reading and rereading the advising manual and the university catalogue, determined to appear authoritative to my new advisees, or at least to keep myself one step ahead of them. In truth, we were all getting oriented together—them to being young adults, me to being a true academic professional.

I also gained a new cooking student. Henry could be held off no longer. My plan had always been to offer Henry the same deal as Jonah, to repeat my series of cooking lessons with him during his final year of high school. Henry was only in eighth grade. But Henry did not want to wait.

Henry had never wanted to wait for anything. His impatience had something to do with having a brother almost five years his senior. Jonah hadn't had a big brother to emulate and never displayed this kind of impatience. Here's my most vivid Baby Jonah memory: At six months old, he sat Buddha-like in front of a big, sturdy Richard Scarry book, open before him on the floor. He carefully turned a page and leaned forward to examine the pictures of Lowly Worm and friends, his eyes moving methodically across the pages. After a moment, he leaned back up and turned the page again, pinching gingerly with his chubby yet graceful fingers. I could have more kids, I thought. If this is what it's like. I could have a *few* more.

Let's just say I never had that thought with Henry. From his intense, lightning-quick birth, he was entirely unlike his mellow big brother. Jonah was four when Henry was born, and we woke him up in the middle of the night so he could watch Henry enter the world. The midwife made notes of Jonah's observations about the birth. Of his red-faced, howling little sibling Jonah said, proudly, "Hey, he's already talking! He's saying 'wow, wow, wow, wow!'" Jonah had other classic comments: "Mom's vagina is messy, but the placenta looks really cool." My friend Jennifer, in attendance to help me during and after the birth, cooked that "cool" placenta for me while I wrestled with little Henry, struggling to get him to latch on and settle down. She sautéed the placenta in olive oil and garlic, and it was perfect. I devoured it. (I guess it only tasted good to me—Jake stopped after one bite). I liked the idea of eating my placenta. I'd read a few radical articles about the health benefits, and they pointed out that all other mammals do it, so why not me? Maybe I also thought it would be fun to tell people that I ate my placenta and observe their shocked reactions (this has, in fact, been fun). But it also really hit the spot.

Henry's birth scene depicts our family in a nutshell, and it's a portrait I'm admittedly fond of: Four-year old Jonah, awake in the middle of the night and, entirely unperturbed, makes astute comments about his screaming, blood-and-shit covered newborn brother Henry, while Jake hovers around sweet and concerned, and I chow down on some garlic placenta.

Once his eyes opened enough to look out into the world, and the screaming slowed down a bit, Henry intently watched Jonah run and play, day after day. He often howled in frustration at his own immobility. At the improbable age of five months, Henry hauled his blobby body onto hands and knees and crawled. Even worse, he stood up at nine months and walked, drunken-sailoring after his big brother and into every sharp corner and hard surface in the world. He *would* catch up, if it killed him. Imagine his poor mother. And especially his poor worrywart father.

Henry's early years had a different feel from Jonah's babyhood, more stable in some ways, less so in others. Our circumstances were ostensibly wilder when Jonah was little—Jake and I were full-time musicians, touring frequently in the Mysteries of Life, with Jonah along for the ride. Still, he had both parents close at hand most of the time, and when I wasn't actually on stage performing he was usually strapped to my body or attached to my breast. By the time Henry was born, Jake was in graduate school and not playing much, while I was still working occasionally as a drummer. I was heading out of town regularly on short tours starting when Henry was around two, leaving Jake with first-grade Jonah and toddling Henry. This was new territory for Jake, and he took his responsibility seriously. Jake was determined to both mother and father our wild little one, and those stretches of time gave Jake and Henry a strong bond. The experience amplified Jake's protective urges and often left him on edge. Tension developed as I settled into a more relaxed role, the in-and-out-the-door parent, the classic "fun dad" role.

Sometimes it was a matter of navigating minor incidents. "Deadly," Jake would snap, finding one of my disposable razors sitting negligently on the rim of the bathtub. He was right, I admitted, I shouldn't leave that sitting there. I'd been much more on the ball when Jonah was little, and although it's universal to lighten up with your second child, I was probably too relaxed.

Some situations were a much bigger deal. Back when we were living in Nottingham, we took a family road trip to Scotland and spent a few days on the Isle of Mull, a beautiful island in the Inner Hebrides. Eight-year-old Henry was an early bird, always up with or before the sun. When he was one, he had a habit of greeting each day by charging outside completely naked and spinning in circles, arms outstretched, a cherubic and ecstatic devotee of the rising sun. So it was no surprise when Henry asked if we could wake up at 6:00 to explore the island, every day, just the two of us, while Jake and Jonah slept in. Henry was a handful at eight. He pushed against every boundary and protested every restriction. He seemed always to be asking questions: "Can I climb that (lion statue, rusty fence, pile of bricks)? Can I go into that (condemned building, mossy pond, head shop)? Can I try this (horseback riding, decrepit rollercoaster, triple hot-fudge sundae)?" And in general we (especially Jake) spouted a litany of "No, no, no." It was exhausting.

I agreed to Henry's request. The early morning walks seemed like an easy way to ease some of the tension, an opportunity to let him run a little wild lest he explode in frustration. It felt good to say "yes" for once.

Mull was amazing in the morning. We poked around the quaint seaside village of Tobermory, along the docks and by the fishing boats. We walked up a long stretch of old stone stairs, up into the residential part of the village, down leafy streets, past cottages and gardens. Eventually we found ourselves on the single road that traversed the whole island, lined with shale cliffs, steep and crumbly. Uh-oh. "Hey," said Henry, eyeing those cliffs. "Can I climb that?" The no rose within me, but I slammed on my internal pause button. I wanted to say yes to him. But. I looked at the cliff in question. How high was it? There appeared to be plenty of secure handholds and footholds. It actually looked very climbable. It wasn't as crumbly as some of the other pieces of cliff we'd passed. But it was steep. It was dangerous, definitely. Was it too dangerous? "Please," said Henry. He was strong, coordinated, and still had some softness, some baby fat to cushion a fall. And I'd be there, I could spot him, help him right away if anything happened. I should say no, I thought.

"OK," I said. "Be so careful."

"I can?" said Henry in disbelief. "Really?"

"Yes," I said. And I could feel the disappointment of a thousand no's evaporate.

Henry climbed, slowly, steadily, with my eyes stuck to him. Before long, he was way, way up there. A couple of cars zoomed by. What must they have thought of this strange scenario? I kept my eyes on Henry as he worked his way down, until he was standing in front of me, out of breath, his big blue eyes even wider than usual. "That," he said, "was the best thing I've ever done. Ever."

I still don't know if I made the right call that day on Mull. If Henry had slipped, if he had fallen, he could have broken a bone or worse. But I'll never forget those looks he gave me, that grateful look when I said yes, and that dazed look after his climb. I could see that space, freedom, and trust were gold to little Henry, and that he would always be impatient for more of all three.

Henry was not only impatient—he was resolute. One night, a couple of years after the Scotland climb, our family went out to dinner and missed the bus back home. It was chilly and damp, and the next bus wasn't due for an hour. The only place open nearby was McDonald's. We've never been a fast food kind of family, and Henry in particular was staunchly anti-Mickey D's. They destroyed rain forests to raise cattle, they employed cruel methods of meat production, and their food was gross and unhealthy. He was a passionate vegetarian at the time. I knew all of this, but I suggested that we take refuge in McDonald's while we waited for the bus. Under the circumstances, it was a reasonable idea, and Jake and Jonah agreed.

"No," said Henry. "I will *not* go in there."

We tried to convince him that it was no big deal, it was just this once. In the end, Jake, Jonah, and I sat at a yellow molded plastic table, warm and dry, drinking ridiculously sweet hot chocolate from polystyrene cups, while Henry stood outside, glaring in at us through the window from beneath the golden arches.

"I can't believe you did that," he said when we walked out. "That is so evil."

Honestly, the whole thing just plain warmed my heart.

So there would be no waiting: Henry and I began cooking lessons. I was grateful. Cooking with Henry would soften the blow of no longer cooking with Jonah. My new job helped me shift into the right mode for new beginnings, which in turn inspired me to start a food blog, a project I'd long contemplated. I set up the blog, with some generous help from a blogging friend, and established "lovesmiths" as a place to document my experiences in the kitchen with Henry. Eventually the blog would shift away from this focus, but it was a great place to start.

For the lessons, I couldn't just copy my approach with Jonah; I needed a fresh start there, too. I knew this new project would work best on Henry's terms, so I let him choose the foods we prepared. I also knew he'd be more interested if we focused on technique rather than recipes. One of our earliest lessons was on how to make a roux-based white sauce. This was perfect—Henry mastered the technique and ran with it, and soon concocted a creamy spinach dip from a white sauce base.

Our biggest success that fall was pesto. Pesto had always been important to Henry and was maybe the primary thing standing between toddler Henry and nutritional deficiency. Pesto was my most successful strategy to sneak green vegetables into his diet. Jonah, the baby road warrior, never needed to be tricked into eating his veggies, and his omnivorousness left us unprepared for Henry. Bereft of the dubious benefit of joining his parents on rock tours, Henry was a more typical toddler regarding food. A picky eater. When friends invited our family over to dinner, they'd ask ahead of time about our kids' preferences.

"Don't bother trying," I'd say. "Jonah will eat anything. Henry will eat nothing."

Henry turned up his nose at most foods, which made it all the weirder when he insisted, at the age of four, that he was a trained chef. Henry was adamant, and Jonah pressed him on it: "Where did you get trained?" Jonah asked. As it turned out, Henry had received his training on the planet "Popy," the home of his imaginary alter-ego, John Mugazin.

"Oh really," continued Jonah, still hoping to come out on top. "If you're a chef, then what's your specialty?"

"Wait," said little Henry. "I'll make it for you."

And so Henry made Jonah his specialty, a little something he called "pop pie," (named for planet Popy) comprising a single Altoid with a slice of bread smushed firmly into a ball around it. Jonah declined to eat his pop pie. Henry was not discouraged, and for months he offered his specialty to everybody. The only taker was his loyal preschool buddy Mackie.

"This is good," said Mackie. He politely requested pop pie every time he came over.

Pop pie didn't do anything to help with Henry's vegetable problem. In particular, he didn't eat enough green vegetables. We tried the classic Popeye argument, but really we were gun-shy about pushing Popeye too hard ever since Jonah, who had perhaps been overexposed to Popeye cartoons when he was littler, had once pounced on an unsuspecting girl at the shopping mall, fists swinging, gleefully singing the words of the Popeye theme song, "I biffs 'em and boffs 'em!" We subdued the usually calm and peaceful Jonah and apologized to the crying little girl and her angry parents. And we cut way back on Popeye cartoons.

Happily, I discovered pesto, a nonviolent solution. Picky Henry loved pesto, and I found I could sneak all kinds of greens into the mix—parsley, spinach, kale, arugula—and he would always eat it.

Thirteen-year-old Henry had outgrown much of his pickiness, but pesto remained a favorite. For our lesson, I kept the instructions loose and I focused instead on the general proportions of cheese/ nuts/salt/greens/pasta. I showed him how to use the food processor, although I was nervous about its extremely sharp blade. He clearly appreciated this gesture. Space, freedom, and trust were still the keys for Henry.

Soon, Henry had invented his signature blend: spinach and Brazil nuts on bow-tie pasta. As the weeks went by, he started to ask, "Do you want me to make pesto for dinner?" It was vaguely reminiscent of those pop pie days gone by. But with a major difference: his pesto was amazing, and yes we *did* want him to make it for dinner. When we praised him lavishly he only shrugged. The achievement came as no surprise to Henry. And we should have been well beyond being surprised by him anymore. "Wow," we said with our mouths full. "Wow, wow, wow."

Spinach and Brazil Nut Pesto

1 cup well-packed fresh spinach leaves

1 cup well-packed fresh basil leaves

⅓ cup olive oil

½ cup Brazil nuts

3 cloves garlic, roughly chopped

¾ cup grated Parmesan or Romano cheese

½ teaspoon salt

1. In a food processor, combine all the ingredients. Pulse to blend. Add water if necessary, 1 tablespoon at a time, to reach desired consistency.

2. Refrigerate, covered, until ready to use. The pesto will keep for 2 weeks in the refrigerator. Serve with cooked pasta or rice, in sandwiches, or on top of grilled chicken or fish.

Vegan Basil Miso Pesto

2 cups basil leaves

⅓ cup pine nuts

½ cup olive oil

2 cloves garlic, coarsely chopped

2 tablespoons mellow white miso

¼ teaspoon salt, or to taste

1. Combine all ingredients in a food processor. Pulse to blend.

2. Refrigerate, covered, until ready to use. The pesto will keep for 2 weeks in the refrigerator. Serve with cooked pasta or rice, in sandwiches, or on top of grilled chicken or fish.

Pistachio Hot Pepper Pesto

1 clove garlic, coarsely chopped

1 jalapeño pepper, seeded and coarsely chopped

2 cups well-packed fresh basil leaves

⅓ cup unsalted pistachios

½ cup Parmesan or Romano cheese

¼ teaspoon salt, or to taste

¼ cup olive oil

2 tablespoons fresh lime juice

1. In a food processor, combine all the ingredients and pulse to blend. Add water, 1 tablespoon at a time, until the desired consistency is reached. Taste and adjust the seasoning as needed.

2. Refrigerate, covered, until ready to use. The pesto will keep for 2 weeks in the refrigerator. Serve with cooked pasta or rice, in sandwiches, or on top of grilled chicken or fish.

Garlic Placenta

2 tablespoons olive oil

1 fresh placenta, chopped into medium bite-sized pieces

2–3 cloves garlic, minced

Salt, to taste

1. In a large skillet over medium heat, warm the olive oil. Add the placenta and garlic and cook, stirring constantly, for a few minutes, until the placenta is medium-rare. Season to taste with salt and eat immediately.

CHAPTER ELEVEN

The Cosmic Muffin

"**Y**OUR APARTMENT SMELLS LIKE MINE DID IN 1973," said my neighbor and landlady, Mary Ellen, as she passed by our open door one Sunday afternoon. I knew what she meant. It wasn't that my apartment smelled like pot or incense. Nothing that sexy or exotic. That seventies smell was maple syrup, cinnamon, toasted nuts, and oats. Henry and I were on a granola kick.

Cooking lessons with Henry had pushed me to find open-ended, technique-based recipes, and granola was perfect. We experimented a lot—Henry was all about the mad-scientist approach in the kitchen—and after making batches of granola that were too sweet, too oily, or too bland, we came up with a perfect, infinitely flexible granola recipe. I posted the recipe on my blog and it quickly became the most popular post at lovesmiths.

During our granola kick, we prepared it most Sundays and packed it into glass jars for the week ahead. Granola was easy, so sometimes we also made a batch of muffins to freeze, including a specialty of mine, the Cosmic Muffin, a flaxseed and bran muffin that I'd developed for Soma, a coffee shop in downtown Bloomington. I'd worked for Soma briefly when I was pregnant with Henry, developing vegan cookie and muffin recipes. The job didn't work out long-term, but you can still buy my almond chocolate chip cookies and Cosmic Muffins at Soma today.

Mary Ellen wasn't the only one in the building reliving the seventies. All this hippie food took me right back to my weird southern Indiana childhood, especially to the years after my parents' divorce, when I lived in Unionville with my mother and brother in a small farmhouse on an acre of land. It was my mom's utopian experiment, complete with gardens, chickens, apple trees, and a wood burning stove. She had a cluster of counter-culture type friends who lived nearby in Bloomington or Needmore, a rural commune. Parties were all-night affairs out in the country, with adults jamming on bluegrass music, rolling joints, and building fires while the kids were skinny dipping, climbing trees, and sneaking beers. When the party moved indoors there was earthy, wholesome food for everybody, like eggplant casseroles, oatmeal cookies, and of course granola.

Bloomington, even in the twenty-first century, still carries strong vestiges of its hippie past. You can buy granola at the co-operative grocery, Bloomingfoods, scooping it from the same bulk bins my mom and her friends used back in the day. Soma, where my Cosmic Muffin is in the case, has an old-school radical vibe— just a bit grimy, as if to say, "Look, we're not catering to the mainstream here. Go to Starbucks if you want clean. Come to Soma if you want cosmic."

But there is a whole other side to my Bloomington, past and present. It is *Southern* Indiana, after all, practically Kentucky. Bloomington is every bit as country as it is hippie, and the country culture of my youth was equally influential in terms of my identity and my approach to music and, of course, food. If granola and bran muffins represent the hippies, biscuits and gravy represents the good ol' boys and girls.

Biscuits and gravy is standard diner food in Indiana and a lifelong favorite of mine. I ate this Hoosier specialty most often during my teen years, when my friends and I frequented diners and greasy spoons in Bloomington. For a couple of dollars you could get a plate of sausage-studded, peppery gravy served over buttermilk biscuits. Another fifty cents would get you a bottomless cup of coffee. We lingered for hours in the booths of these places, smoking cigarettes, doing homework, and playing our favorites in the jukeboxes. Each place had a distinctive jukebox record—"Louie Louie," "Me and Bobby McGee," "Beast of Burden," "Red Red Wine." I can taste the bad coffee and salty gravy just thinking about these songs. I think of biscuits and gravy as a quintessentially Indiana thing. In fact, one of the most beloved bands of my high school years, Bloomington punk band the Gizmos, had a song called "Biscuits and Gravy" that starts out, "I used to live in Indiana..."

My love of biscuits and gravy has even deeper roots that lead even deeper south. My paternal grandmother, Violet, from Nashville, Tennessee, was the best cook I've ever known. Her biscuits, in particular, were a miracle. Violet was kind and undemanding. She rarely asked for anything, but the story goes that when my mother announced her pregnancy with me, Violet (the mother of three sons) made a direct request: "Have a girl." Right after I was born, my mother plopped little bundled-up me into my grandmother's arms. "Violet," she said, "I had you that girl." That girl had Violet from then on. She adored me.

It was mutual. When I was four, my parents left me with Violet for a week. We picked okra and green tomatoes from her garden and fried them, coated in cornmeal. We cut biscuits from the feathery dough she created, then stirred milk and sausage into a smooth gravy. She served me "milky coffee"—a half-teaspoon of Sanka, a couple teaspoons of sugar, and a lot of milk—and I felt happy and grown-up, sitting and sipping with her at her Formica kitchen table. Going back home after that was a letdown. No more doting, no more biscuits, no more coffee. I was deeply insulted when my parents insisted I take a bath before bed; I cracked completely, jumped out of the bathtub, charged dripping down the hall to my bedroom, leapt onto my rocking horse and began to rock furiously. "I'm going back to Grandma's!" I yelled.

I have her to thank for my love of food. She had a way with simple ingredients, even things nobody else bothered with. One time when she visited us in Indiana, she took me to a big public park full of crabapple trees. The ground was covered with the ugly little fruits, of interest only to bugs and squirrels. And Violet. "We can make jelly out of these," she said. I was amazed. We collected a big bag full of ripe little apples—not the green ones, she told me, and not the brown ones—and back in our kitchen, with barely any other ingredients (sugar, I think was the only other component) we made a big pot of crabapple jelly and sealed it into sterilized Mason jars. She went back to Nashville and I was sad, but she left behind those jars of crimson jelly, and every morning I asked for crabapple jelly on my toast.

I saw less of Violet during my teen years and twenties, but she remained a steadfast force of unconditional love. She must have been surprised when her little granddaughter became a rock drummer, but she was never anything but sweet and encouraging. When Antenna had a show in Nashville, we all stayed at her house. Some of my most endearing tour memories involve hanging out and sharing food with my bandmates' families. There's something about having dinner with somebody's dad that helps you get to know that somebody in a whole new way. I liked that. And doing the family hang tends to bring everybody down to earth in a healthy way. During a two-day stopover in Erie at the home of Juliana's father, Phil, he insisted that we partake of his hobby at the time, baking bread. We spent an entire day in his big suburban kitchen, up to our elbows in flour. During a trip through Washington DC, Paul Strohm blew our minds by taking us out for Ethiopian food, a whole new experience for all of us. In San Francisco, we crashed with John's brother Jake in his amazing rent-controlled apartment in the Mission, and he introduced us to California-style burritos, stuffed with brown rice and black beans. They immediately became our favorite food.

In Nashville, we stayed with Violet: Jake, John, and our road manager, Nick, a big, burly tattooed guy who would have startled most grandmothers. Not mine. She welcomed us all, and cooked an incredible spread: fried chicken, greens, chocolate pie, and of course biscuits. She even made extra biscuits and packed them up for us in Ziploc bags. It wasn't until we were in the van, heading down the highway, when Nick finally tasted his first Violet biscuit. "Oh my god," he said, "these are the best biscuits I've ever had. In my life." Yep. Best ones he'll ever have, guaranteed.

I reconnected with Violet during my months at the Kushi Institute. Something about being there, living and breathing food, inspired me to be more in touch with her. I also had more time to myself than I'd ever had—no band, no drama. Violet and I became pen pals. I confided in her about my conflicting feelings about the next stage of my life. Would I go back to college? Or go back to playing music? Was I too young to get married and have babies with Jake? Whatever I did would be right in her eyes, she told me; she simply urged me to be happy. As it turned out, I would be married and pregnant with Jonah within a year of those letters.

She was the first person I called, positive home pregnancy test in hand. After Jonah was born, she stayed with us for ten days, helping in every way possible: cleaning, changing diapers, sleeping with Jonah so I could rest more deeply. And cooking. She made whatever I wanted. Chicken and dumplings, bean soup, pasta salad. I've never felt more nurtured in my life, and this adoring attention eased my transition into motherhood. This is what love looks like, she seemed to say with every quiet gesture and every plate of food. This is how you take care of people. This is how you show support, how you engender trust, happiness, and security. Freda, she said without saying, this is how to be a mother.

The Cosmic Muffin, biscuits, granola: these foods all link me to people and places and times in my life. The Cosmic Muffin still connects me to Bloomington, and to my various attempts at a baking career. Furthermore, it's a creation that would never have existed if I hadn't had instilled in me by Violet, almost from birth, the pleasures of baking and feeding.

Violet died the summer that Jonah and I started his cooking lessons. Soon after she died, I ceremoniously made biscuits and gravy, an evolving vegetarian version I'd been tweaking for years. I shared the meal with Jonah and Henry, and talked to them about their great-grandmother. I wanted to keep her alive in their minds, to link her with biscuits so strongly that they will think of her whenever they bake and eat biscuits. I won't have to try to do this for myself. Whenever I make them, I think of her. What about granola? Will Henry think of me when he makes it thirty years from now, maybe with his own kids, or forty years from now, when his kids are in college, or fifty years from now, when I will surely be gone? Cosmic, indeed.

Vegetarian Biscuits and Gravy

Serves 4

For the Biscuits

2 cups self-rising flour

½ cup shortening or 1 stick unsalted butter

⅔ cup buttermilk plus 1–2 tablespoons, if needed

For the Gravy

2 cups whole milk or unsweetened soy milk

1 tablespoon soy sauce

1 teaspoon dried sage

1 teaspoon dried thyme

½ teaspoon salt

Big pinch ground white pepper

Pinch cayenne pepper, optional

3 tablespoons olive oil

14-ounce package vegetarian ground sausage, chopped into small bite-sized pieces

⅓ cup all-purpose flour

To Make the Biscuits

1. Preheat the oven to 425°F.

2. In a large bowl, work the shortening into the flour with your fingers or a fork, quickly and lightly. The mixture should have the consistency of coarse meal. (You can also pulse in a food processor a few times, then transfer to a large bowl.)

3. Slowly stir in the buttermilk, until the dough comes together. If the flour isn't completely incorporating, add a couple more tablespoons of buttermilk, 1 tablespoon at a time.

RECIPE CONTINUES

4. Turn the dough out onto a floured surface, fold and knead brief-ly, and press into a ½-inch-thick rectangle. It can be a little thicker.

5. Using a biscuit cutter, cut rounds. Place the rounds on an un-greased baking sheet, with the edges just touching. Bake for 10 to 12 minutes, until golden brown.

To Make the Gravy

1. In a medium bowl, whisk together the milk or soymilk with 1 cup of water and the soy sauce, sage, thyme, salt, pepper, and cayenne pepper, if using. Set aside.

2. In a deep, wide skillet over medium heat, warm the olive oil. Add the sausage and brown, stirring constantly, for 5 minutes. Add the flour, reduce the heat to medium-low, and stir for 2 to 3 minutes.

3. Gradually whisk in the milk mixture, then whisk more to fully combine. Bring to a boil, stirring constantly, then reduce heat to low and cook for 15 minutes. Taste and adjust the seasoning as needed. To serve, split the biscuits open and top with warm gravy.

Fried Green Tomatoes

Serves 4–6

4 medium green tomatoes, cut into ¼-inch slices

Salt, to taste

Freshly ground black pepper, to taste

⅓ cup all-purpose flour

2 tablespoons cornmeal

¼ cup canola oil

1. Season the tomato slices generously on both sides with salt and pepper.

2. In a shallow bowl, combine the flour and cornmeal. Drag the tomato slices through the mixture to coat each side thoroughly. Shake off any excess.

3. In a heavy skillet over medium heat, warm the oil until it is hot but not smoking. Fry the tomatoes in batches, about 4 minutes on each side. Transfer to a plate lined with paper towels. Serve hot.

Maple–Peanut–Cacao Granola

This variation evolved out of the basic recipe that Henry and I developed. The addition of cacao nibs, peanuts, and pumpkin seeds was directly inspired by our huge obsession with Rick Bayless's Xoco Granola. Our version is sweetened with maple syrup instead of the honey and sugar in the Xoco blend. I love the richness and mellow sweetness that the maple syrup brings.

Makes approximately 5½ cups

2 tablespoons coconut oil, plus more for oiling

½ cup maple syrup

1 teaspoon cinnamon

1 teaspoon vanilla extract

½ teaspoon salt

3 cups old-fashioned rolled oats

¾ cup roasted, salted peanuts

¾ cup raw pumpkin seeds

½ cup raw cacao nibs

½ cup raisins

1. Preheat the oven to 300°F. Lightly oil a baking dish—either a rimmed cookie sheet or a 13 × 9-inch dish. Set aside.

2. In a large, deep skillet over medium heat, melt the coconut oil. Add the maple syrup, cinnamon, vanilla, and salt. Stir well. Add the oats, peanuts, and pumpkin seeds. Stir constantly for 1 minute or so to completely coat and lightly toast nuts and seeds.

3. Remove from the heat and transfer the mixture to the prepared baking dish, spreading the granola out evenly in a thin layer. Bake 30 to 40 minutes, stirring every 10 minutes, until toasty and brown. Add the cacao nibs and raisins after 25 minutes of baking. Cool completely and store in a sealed container.

The Cosmic Muffin

I lost the recipe and all my notes for The Cosmic Muffin ("how very hippie-ish of you," pointed out a friend), so it took some work to try to recreate the muffin I invented 15 years ago. In the process, I updated the recipe to include coconut oil and coconut sugar, rather than the canola oil and maple syrup used in the original. I kept the oat bran, flax seed, and heroic dose of ground ginger.

Makes 16–18 muffins

1 cup soy milk or almond milk

1 tablespoon apple cider vinegar

¾ cup canned pumpkin purée

½ cup melted and slightly cooled coconut oil

1 tablespoon vanilla extract

¾ cup oat bran

¼ cup ground flaxseed

1½ cups unbleached white flour

¾ cup coconut sugar

1 tablespoon baking powder

1 scant tablespoon ground ginger

1 teaspoon ground cinnamon

1 teaspoon salt

¼ teaspoon ground nutmeg

½ cup raisins

1 cup coarsely chopped walnuts, optional

1. Preheat the oven to 400°F. Line enough muffin tins with paper cups to make 16–18 muffins.

2. In a medium bowl, combine the soy or almond milk and apple cider vinegar. Allow the mixture to curdle for 1 minute or so, then whisk in the pumpkin puree, coconut oil, and vanilla. Stir in the oat bran and flaxseed and set aside for a few minutes.

RECIPE CONTINUES

3. In a large bowl, whisk together the flour, sugar, baking powder, ginger, cinnamon, salt, and nutmeg. Add the wet ingredients to the dry ingredients, using as few strokes as possible to combine. Fold in the raisins and walnuts, if using.

4. Fill each muffin cup a little over ¾ full. Bake for 24 to 26 minutes, until a toothpick inserted in the center of a muffin comes out clean. Let cool in the pans for 2 to 3 minutes, then transfer to wire racks to let cool completely.

CHAPTER TWELVE

Huevos Jonah

J ONAH WAS HOME from the University of Illinois for the
weekend. Again. He'd travelled back to Evanston that fall
more than I had expected. He missed his friends, he missed Chicago, he missed healthy home-cooked meals, and he missed the
privacy of his own room. I didn't blame him, and I was always
glad to see him. The frequent visits made it easier to adjust to his
being gone and made those months feel like a period of transition rather than a cold, sharp break. But the frequent visits also
made it harder to adjust. It took me only an instant to fall back
into the familiar routine, with two sons under one roof. Then
Sunday would come and I'd have to say goodbye again, and that
adjustment was never instant.

Jonah had taken to making his own breakfast on his weekends at home, usually over-easy eggs topped with salsa, jalapeño peppers, avocado, and whatever else he could dig out of the fridge. I liked to see him whipping up a hearty meal for himself, and I appreciated his comfort and confidence in the kitchen, although I lamented the lack of variety in his concoctions. He kept making that same egg thing, again and again.

It wasn't fair for me to judge him, though, since I'd had an egg rut of my own when I was his age.

Mine started when my mother's new husband, Ahmet, concocted a fantastic breakfast for our family in Bloomington right before I moved to Boston and my mom and Ahmet moved to Turkey. Ahmet separated a bunch of eggs, scrambled the whites in butter with feta cheese and oregano, nested the yolks into the scramble, and covered the skillet to cook on low. He served it in generous slices with hunks of bakery bread on the side. After a lifetime of the same old eggs, it was a whole new experience: salty feta, zingy oregano, creamy egg yolks.

I immediately replicated the recipe and named it "Eggs Ahmet." Eggs Ahmet was almost as easy to put together as the scrambled eggs I'd mastered as a child, but it was full of enough surprises to make scrambled eggs interesting again. I cooked the dish again and again. In my first apartment in Boston, it was my go-to breakfast. And then often my go-to dinner. I loved making the dish for myself, but it was the most fun to cook for other people, to watch their surprise and delight. "You should open a restaurant," said my roommate Anne. Eggs Ahmet was another early lesson in the value of welcoming outside influences into the kitchen. I eventually snapped out of my particular egg rut; Eggs Ahmet fell by the wayside years later when I learned how to make a proper omelet.

That's what I decided Jonah should do. To break out of his rut, he should make himself an omelet. I suggested this, and the moment the words left my mouth I realized that I'd never taught Jonah this basic skill. How had I skipped what should have been one of our first cooking lessons? Instead, it would be one of our last. We agreed on an October Sunday-morning meeting in the kitchen before his bus trip back to Champaign.

The agreed-upon morning arrived. The eggs and mushrooms sat on the counter. They sat there for a very long while. I looked at the clock. All gentle attempts to wake Jonah with reasonable knocks on his door had failed, and I wasn't willing to escalate my efforts. I wanted to pound and yell. But I wasn't going to.

This would have been a good time to recall that for years I had longed for this moment, when my children would sleep past 6:00 in the morning. Back on those bleary mornings, with toddler Jonah pulling on my arm before sunrise, I thought, "Someday maybe this kid will sleep in. I'll sleep in. I'll wake up whenever I want. I'll pull on *his* arm." I completely believed that I would welcome the role reversal. Mostly, I have.

Alas, I was smack in the middle of an existential parenting crisis, and my good night of sleep was beside the point. The point was, I had very little authority over my son anymore. This was right and natural. It was also maddening and uncomfortable. I wasn't sure what to do with myself, so I banged around the apartment.

"What's wrong?" said Henry.

"Oh nothing," I said, in another odd moment of role reversal, with me in the role of the pouty, uncommunicative teenager. "I *was* going to teach Jonah how to make an omelet."

"Can *I* make an omelet?" Asked Henry. *Of course.*

"No," I said

But he asked again and again and I relented. I may even have smiled beneath my sighs.

"Here," I said, handing him a recipe. "Read through this and get all the ingredients together. Let me know when you're ready and I'll help you in the kitchen."

I retreated to my bedroom to compose myself, stretching out to read the newspaper. Maybe the morning could turn itself around without me.

Mornings have often been a weird and lonely time for me. I was the early riser in the Blake Babies. When we were on tour and staying in hotels, I'd wake up and tiptoe around our hotel room, silently get dressed, and then head to the lobby for a cup of coffee, embark upon a five-or-so-mile run, eat breakfast at the Denny's next door (there was always a Denny's next door), and read *USA Today* (free at the Red Roof Inn, where we often stayed). Finally I'd get bored and go sit on the edge of John's bed with my fourth cup of coffee, chattering to him non-stop until he'd eventually groan, roll over, and get up. Not every morning was like this on Blake Babies tours, but many mornings were.

My morning routine was much more uncomfortable when we stayed in people's houses. I acquired the habit of riffling through our hosts' kitchens. I tended to wake up ravenously hungry, sometimes dizzy, and couldn't stand to wait for the stragglers to awaken and head out to breakfast, which sometimes meant no food until noon.

So I riffled.

I figured nobody would mind if I helped myself to a big bowl of Wheaties or a tall glass of juice. I liked seeing what kind of food people kept in their kitchens, and was intrigued by anything unfamiliar to me: sweet flavored coffees, marshmallow fluff, peanut butter and jelly swirled together in one jar. I must admit, I enjoyed riffling—years later I'd be exploring the kitchens at the Kushi Institute, stealing bites of fresh amazake, inspired by the same mildly criminal impulse.

Henry Rollins had the very best kitchen I ever riffled through. The Blake Babies stayed a few nights with him in Venice, California, during a tour in 1989. Our booking agent, who also represented

Rollins, had arranged everything, knowing full well that we were huge admirers of Hank, both thrilled and intimidated by the prospect of being hosted by one of our idols. None of us had met him.

I tried to drum hard and solid at our show in Los Angeles, feeling under pressure to impress the industry-heavy audience. I looked up from my drums, into the crowd, and there was the unmistakable, god-like form of Rollins, painfully beautiful, standing right in front of the stage with his sculpted arms crossed, looking directly at me. I panicked.

My right drumstick flew out of my hand and across the stage, directly towards him. It didn't hit him. Not quite. And of course he never flinched. After a moment of flustered fumbling, I located a back-up stick and fell back into the groove of the song. So much for making an impression.

After the show, Rollins introduced himself, and confirmed the details of our stay with him. That night we set up camp at his house—Juliana in the back bedroom, John and I on a comfortable pullout sofa bed in the living room.

I woke up early, as usual, and tiptoed around the living room and kitchen of his immaculate vintage bungalow. A big stack of meal-replacement bars, the kind from the health food store, sat neatly on the kitchen counter. These were a particular weakness of mine at the time, and I was ravenous. So I inhaled one. It was great. Then I heard a rustle from the next room—Hank was an early riser too!

I instantly felt embarrassed and guilty about my bar thievery, and dove back into the sofa bed next to sleeping John. I closed my eyes and pretended to be asleep while Rollins came out into the kitchen and made coffee. I periodically peeked at him through one eye, and noticed him frowning at the pile of bars; could he tell that one was missing?

I thought about confessing right then, but I was too shy, too in awe, and couldn't muster up the guts. The moment passed.

Hank bellowed from the kitchen at John and me, "Y'all are American, right? You drink coffee, don't you?"

John and I sat up in bed. "Yes," we whispered.

We shuffled out of bed and drank strong, dark coffee with Henry Rollins. It was really, really good coffee.

Over the course of our stay, we grew much less terrified. In fact those were fun days, and he was an entertaining and generous host. We sat on the wooden floor of his study, listening dutifully to the Albert Ayler records he played us. We talked about writing— he was writing a lot at the time, tour diaries, poetry—and he harangued us about how totally and completely he swore by Strunk and White's *The Elements of Style*. We ate it all up. I was at the peak of my running obsession, and he was very into weightlifting, so we found a scrap of common ground as obsessive exercisers.

One night I went out for a run around Venice and was gone a long while—I ran nine miles. When I returned, Hank was visibly impressed.

"You were running all that time?" he asked.

It didn't quite make up for the flying drumstick. But it helped a little.

He took us out to a few different restaurants in Venice. Oh, the food in California!

California is paradise to a touring musician, with its year-round abundance of produce and its strong food culture. California was a reward for surviving the whole middle part of the US. I loved the food out there, all green and healthy and hip.

Everywhere we went, Rollins always ordered the same thing: huevos rancheros. Yep, Hank had an egg rut too.

I had a new Henry in my life now, and mine was no less intense.

After about twenty minutes of relaxing with the newspaper and simmering down, I wondered what had happened to my son's demands for an omelet lesson. Probably he'd forgotten about it and moved onto some other project. Nope. He hadn't moved on.

I found Henry in the dining room, sitting down with a perfect cheese omelet.

"What?" I said.

"I just followed the recipe," he said. "It was easy."

My usual Henry-related feelings: pride, a smidgeon of exasperation. Pride, mostly.

It was getting late and there wasn't much time before Jonah's bus departure. Henry had left most of the omelet ingredients scattered around the kitchen, and I made a decision—I'd make Jonah an omelet. He should have something to eat before he left, after all. I chopped mushrooms and made a rich, sherry-laced sauce, well seasoned with dill. Jonah was up and showered in time to sit down to his favorite kind of omelet.

On that day of changing emotions I'd landed at last in a good place, feeling nothing but motherly satisfaction, watching my son appreciatively dig into his breakfast.

I'd teach him how to make an omelet someday. Or not.

I remembered sitting with a friend and our kids when Jonah was a tiny toddler.

We watched them greedily devour smushed-up bits of banana.

"It's weirdly and deeply gratifying, just watching them eat, isn't it?" said my friend.

"Yes," I replied. "It really is."

Eggs Ahmet

Serves 4

8 eggs

1 tablespoon dried oregano

Big pinch freshly ground black pepper

Pinch salt

2 tablespoons unsalted butter

4 ounces feta cheese

1. Separate the egg yolks from the whites. Let the yolks sit in their shells, let the whites fall into a medium bowl.

2. Combine the whites. Add the oregano, pepper, and salt, and whisk with a fork or wire whisk until well blended and frothy. Set aside.

3. In a large skillet with a lid, over medium heat, warm the butter. Add the egg-white mixture. Crumble the feta on top and gently stir to combine. Add the intact egg yolks, gently nesting them in, trying to evenly space them across the egg whites.

4. Cover and cook for 10 to 12 minutes, until the eggs are set. Slice and serve immediately.

Sherried Mushroom Omelet

Here's what my tester had to say about this: "1. I would never have put this many mushrooms in an omelet. 2. I will now always put this many mushrooms in an omelet. So good!"

Serves 2

For the Filling

2 tablespoons butter or olive oil, divided

1 pound field mushrooms, sliced

1 clove garlic, minced

2 tablespoons dry sherry

1 tablespoon all-purpose flour

¼ cup full-fat Greek yogurt or sour cream

½ teaspoon salt

¼ teaspoon freshly ground black pepper

¼ teaspoon dried dill

For the Omelets

6 eggs, divided

2 tablespoons cream or half-and-half, divided

Salt, to taste

Ground white pepper, to taste

2 tablespoons unsalted butter, divided

To Make the Filling

1. In a large, deep skillet, melt the butter (or warm the oil). Add the mushrooms and cook over medium heat for 5 to 7 minutes, until mushrooms release their juices and the liquid starts to cook off a little. Add the garlic and sherry and continue to cook

RECIPE CONTINUES

for 3 to 4 minutes. Stir in the flour. Cook, stirring constantly to absorb the liquid and lightly toast the flour, 1 to 2 minutes. Add the yogurt, salt, pepper, and dill. Taste and adjust the seasoning as needed. Remove from the heat and set aside.

To Make the Omelets

1. In a blender, combine 3 of the eggs, 1 tablespoon of the cream or half-and-half, and a generous pinch each salt and white pepper. Blend well for 1 minute. Set aside.

2. Warm an 8-inch, nonstick skillet over medium heat. Add 1 tablespoon of the butter and swirl the skillet to coat. Do not let the butter brown.

3. Add the egg mixture and scrape down the side of the pan with a rubber spatula so the eggs cook evenly. When the mixture is somewhat set, but still wet (this only takes about 30 or so seconds!), smooth the top with the spatula, checking that the thickness is fairly even.

4. Cover ½ of the omelet with ½ of the mushroom mixture, spreading the filling out evenly. Using the rubber spatula, lift the non-filling side up over the filling side, to fold the omelet in half.

5. Slide the omelet onto a plate. Repeat all the steps to cook the second omelet. Serve immediately.

CHAPTER THIRTEEN

Solo Flights and Empty Nests

I HAVE A FAVORITE PHOTO of Jonah and me. He's around eleven months old, nursing, clutching a hunk of bread that he's sticking into my mouth. He looks like he's trying not to crack up. He looks completely amused, as if he's thinking, "How funny! I'm feeding you, and you're feeding me!" Jonah's joke is funny because, as all parents know, it doesn't usually go both ways.

But a year of lessons with Jonah and my continued experiments with Henry had helped to reverse the feeding flow on occasion. Some of these occasions had become family legend, like Jonah's triumphant chicken dinner and Henry's party-stealing cupcakes. Other occasions passed with less fanfare but were spectacular nonetheless, like the time Jonah made pasta fagioli.

Jake was out of town. It had been a tiring weekend of solo parenting, hearkening back to earlier years, when Jake was sometimes on the road with the Vulgar Boatmen or the Mysteries of Life, who played with an alternate drummer when it was too much to pack the whole family into an RV. During these times, I'd hold down the fort at home with little Jonah. I did a pretty good job of holding down the fort, but meal preparation was my weakness. I'd start strong and determined, cooking full meals, assigning Jonah simple kitchen tasks like peeling carrots, folding napkins, and setting the table. As the days passed, my gumption declined. By day three or four I'd be slapping spoons and bowls on the table with a carton of soymilk and a box of cornflakes. "Cereal for dinner!" I'd declare, trying to make it sound fun.

Of course, solo parenting my largely self-sufficient teenagers was much easier than looking after a little toddler. But this particular weekend had been long. I was tired of being a chauffeur, tired of shopping and cooking, tired of cleaning and washing. By Sunday night, I could easily have been convinced to offer cornflakes for dinner. Instead, I handed Jonah a recipe for pasta fagioli that I'd adapted from *The Sopranos Cookbook*. "Please," I said, "make this later?"

"Yep, sure," said Jonah, unfazed.

Henry had outgrown all his clothes overnight, so I took him shopping while Jonah prepared dinner. When we trudged back into the house, faint with hunger, heavy with shopping bags, the house smelled incredible, full of the scents of olive oil, garlic, and tomatoes. Jonah unconsciously turned the tables by asking me to fold the napkins and set the table. And he set out three bowls filled with hot pasta and white beans in a garlicky red sauce. It was better than cornflakes. It was better than anything.

Way back when I'd first thought about a year of cooking lessons with Jonah, I'd thought that when the year was over, his childhood would be over. I'd attached heavy significance to the moment when he'd cross a threshold. Perhaps that was a way to prepare myself. And then the moment surged into view. And then it arrived. And I wasn't ready. Not at all.

In the final weeks before we drove Jonah to the University of Illinois, we didn't cook together as much. We shopped and packed and planned. It was during this stretch that I got the happy phone call about the academic advisor position, and I cried with relief about my new job. Only a few years earlier I'd been working at a health food store in England for minimum wage. Now I had a faculty position at Northwestern. My salary wasn't amazing, but it was decent and combined with Jake's would make it possible for us to help Jonah, and to minimize the amounts we'd all have to borrow. There was a long way to go, but I could glimpse a future free of Sallie Mae. A distant future, but there. While Jonah packed to cross the threshold, we were moving in the right direction.

I was quietly crossing a threshold of my own. I had no more cover letters to write, no more résumés to post; my interminable job search was over. I was out of survival mode, ready to exhale, ready to live my life. I missed playing music. It had been six years since I'd played—my longest hiatus by far. I'd quit Antenna to run off to the Kushi Institute, and I'd quit again when I was first pregnant with Jonah, but those turned out to be short breaks. In the few years before we moved to England, I played in more bands than at any other stage of my life. There were original local bands Gentleman Caller and Lola; a post-Blake Babies project with Juliana Hatfield, Some Girls; and a hard-working cover band out of Bedford, Indiana, 24/7.

During our four years in Nottingham, I played a grand total of two shows—one with Jake as the Mysteries of Life, opening for the Lemonheads, and the other as part of Juliana's rhythm section for a show in London. I looked at my break from music as a chance to search out new pursuits, a search that led me to

an evening class in creative writing at the University of Nottingham. That class, led by British writer Anthony Cropper, changed
everything for me. Every week we played weird experimental
writing games, making up stories about randomly selected photographs or inserting arbitrary sentences into the middle of a piece
of prose to see what happened. We read tons of great writers, too,
like Amy Hempel and Alice Munro, writers I now can't imagine
living without. I started writing stories myself and published a
few in small UK publications. Writing was the perfect thing for
me then; I was lonely in a foreign country, and here was something I could do alone. I'd always been a reader and I had long
been attracted to writing. In a short autobiography (I wrote it at
the age of nine), I said that when I grew up I wanted to be a "poet
and a scientist." And I'd loved the process of songwriting. I did a
little of that in the Blake Babies and a few of my other bands, but
my limits as a musician usually meant I had to rely on a guitar
player to help me translate my ideas. I didn't need anybody to
help me write short stories, although I benefitted tremendously
from the feedback I received from Cropper and my other teachers, as well as fellow writing students. I kept taking classes, kept
working on stories, and it soon seemed like the most logical thing
to apply to graduate school and complete a master's in creative
writing. During a meeting with the late Graham Joyce, my thesis
director, I wondered if writing was something I could really do.
Graham said to me directly and unequivocally (oh boy, he'd have
hated those adverbs), "Freda, *you can do this.*" Those words were
like magic. A few years later, I sent him an email about a weird
idea I had for a book about teaching my kids how to cook. "I love
it!" he wrote back.

By the time we were preparing to move back to the States, I
was in a mental place far away from the backstage rooms of Indiana bars. My break from music had served me well, and I felt like I
had found something besides drumming to do. For many years in

Bloomington I'd worked as a yoga teacher, which was direct evolution of my healthy and healing months at the Kushi Institute. I'd wondered sometimes if teaching yoga was what I really ought to do for a living. I could plan and teach a decent yoga class, I loved the practice, and people liked my instruction. It felt like a beneficial service and a good livelihood. But it never felt fully satisfying to me. There was some element missing; teaching yoga was creative and performative, but it didn't take me to the extremes that playing music did. Writing did, though. It brought the whole spectrum, and it was something I wanted to be doing for the rest of my life.

Even still, I felt the tug of music, and felt myself circling back around to it once again. While my nest was just about to become half empty, I went to Amazon.com without thinking much about it and ordered a pair of drum brushes. My drum set was down in the basement storage room of our apartment building, having been dragged across the ocean and back. It was getting rusty. But it was there. I felt optimistic.

All of this carried me though August with enough energy to help Jonah prepare. And then, on the day itself, I just plain fell apart. Jonah had packed his bags and boxes into our car, along with the massive, ancient television that he'd bought on Craigslist for twenty bucks. The boys milled around outside. Jake and I moved wordlessly through the apartment, turning off lights, checking for missed items. Jake picked up his acoustic guitar and began to play and sing an old Mysteries of Life song, "Kira's Coming Over." He'd written it when I was first pregnant, a sweet song anticipating Jonah's birth. I went woozy at the sound of it, gripped the edge of our sofa with both hands, and exploded in tears. Like a cartoon character. Jake stopped playing.

"What?" he said.

"No." I said, struggling to speak. "Not that song."

Jake put the guitar down, hugged me tight, and I cried it out as quickly as I could. I didn't have time to wallow. It was time to go.

"It goes so fast," everybody says. I'd heard this uttered from the very moment I became a parent. And now the only thing to say was it went. So fast.

I have a bad habit of wrenching things into compartments, though. I viewed Jonah's departure for college as the end of his childhood. And it *was* that, kind of. Yet there were steps both forward and backward in the years ahead. All through his freshman year at Illinois he returned for all those weekends, and not much had changed. He was still a kid. And the following summer, he would be back, baking scones and bread with me, dreaming of a career as a cigar ambassador, cooking chickens at Whole Foods, until summer ended and there we'd be all over again, packing the car on a hot morning in August, moving Jonah into another dorm, this time in Chicago, this time to the college he would love, the one he would stick with. The following summer, he wouldn't live at home at all, but would rent a house in the city with three friends and would work full-time at a busy restaurant in the Loop, making smoothies, wraps, and burritos for the lunch crowd. Part of me wanted to delineate Jonah's transitions, but it couldn't be done very neatly.

The end of my oldest son's childhood extended almost invisibly over years until it occurred to me one day that he was twenty years old. He had a job. He was more than halfway through college. With some help from us he was paying his rent and his bills, and buying groceries. And he was cooking for himself every day.

"What do you cook the most?" I asked him.

"Some combination of rice, beans, and vegetables, usually," answered Jonah. "Or stir-fry."

Mission accomplished? Maybe not. Probably not. But somewhere along the way, with plenty of stops and starts, Jonah had
crossed a major threshold.

Stops and starts. Steps forward and backward. There's no better way to describe my musical career. "You know," said a drum
teacher to me many years ago, when he found out I was also a yoga
teacher, "there's not the 'you' that does yoga and the 'you' that
plays drums. It's all *you*." He was just trying to get me to relax. I
found his scolding irritating. I didn't like his observation, because
it cut right to the core of a lifelong struggle of mine: my tendency
to split my life and identity into discrete categories. By the time
Jonah had started his sophomore year in Chicago, those nice new
drum brushes had collected a year of dust. While Jake waited out
the terrible tenure process, I worked hard in my first year as an
advisor, Jonah started college and then changed his mind, and
Henry made pesto and white sauce, those brushes remained un-
touched. My drums grew another year of rust. Music retreated
into the distant past. Maybe that was OK, I thought, maybe it was
time to finally let that part of me go. Time to draw a line. After all,
I like to draw lines.

And so I wrenched my musical career to a definite finish, or
so I thought. I sold my drums, the ones I'd played for fifteen years,
the ones I'd dragged across the ocean and back. I sold them on
eBay. It was easy. Until they were gone, and then I felt an emp-
tiness somewhat akin to the feeling I'd had when, in those early
weeks, I'd stood in the doorway of Jonah's clean, vacant bedroom.
But unlike Jonah, my drums were never coming back. They were
gone. Drumming was over.

Until it wasn't. I'd given Jonah a hard time about changing his mind,
but hadn't he come by that trait honestly? I don't know exactly

how it happened. I started to go out to see bands in Chicago and was moved and inspired by everything I heard. Janet Bean, Jon Langford, Nora O'Connor, Kelly Hogan—Chicago was crawling with ridiculously talented performers. I made a few new friends, and I connected with a few old ones from back in my rock days. And somehow, without really trying, I became a drummer again. Less than a year after I'd sold my drums I was on stage performing with my favorite Chicago musician, Robbie Fulks. Not long after that, the Mysteries of Life were recording a new record and playing the occasional show. A musical future looked like a possibility again. It was no big deal to buy new drums. But maybe, I thought, I should stop drawing all these lines, for myself and my kids.

Before Jonah left for college for the second time, I recruited both of my sons to help me make a big, festive dinner for friends. The meal was centered on a roasted poblano and white bean chili I was making. Jonah had become a master of guacamole and salsa fresca since he made gallons of both every day at Whole Foods, and he agreed to whip some up for the meal. Henry had become interested in cheese and very skilled at the stove top, so I put him in charge of grilled quesadillas. It was tight in our little kitchen, but I didn't care. We three concentrated well on our tasks, and I offered not one single tip or scrap of instruction to either of them. They were nineteen and fourteen. They didn't need my help at this particular moment. It goes so fast. But that evening, nothing went fast. We chopped and peeled and tasted in the hot kitchen, as though in slow motion. We wrecked the kitchen completely with no worries or fears (we knew Jake would be there to clean up our mess later), and we put an extraordinary feast on the table, the fruits of just about any literal and metaphorical harvest you could think of. It was one last meal, prepared by a team of equals. It was, I hoped, the first of many meals prepared that way. It was the perfect ending. It was the perfect beginning.

Pasta Fagioli

Serves 8. I wanted a big batch so we'd have leftovers for lunch—you can halve it if you want.

6 tablespoons olive oil

4 stalks celery, chopped

4–6 cloves garlic, minced

1 28-ounce can chopped tomatoes

2 tablespoons tomato paste

1 teaspoon salt

¼ teaspoon ground cayenne pepper

4 15-ounce cans white beans (cannellini or great northern), drained

16 ounces small pasta (bow ties, fusilli, spaghetti broken into 1-inch pieces, anything)

Minced fresh parsley, for serving

Grated Parmesan, for serving

1. In a large pot over medium-low heat, warm the olive oil. Add the celery and garlic and cook, stirring frequently, for 10 minutes. Add the tomatoes, tomato paste, salt, cayenne pepper, and 4 cups of water. Bring to a boil and then simmer for 10 minutes, stirring occasionally.

2. Add the beans and stir for 5 minutes, mashing some of the beans with the back of a spoon to thicken the sauce.

3. Add the pasta and cook for 10 minutes or so, stirring constantly, until the pasta is tender. The mixture will be very thick; add a little more water if you need to. Cover the pot and let stand for 10 minutes. Serve immediately topped with parsley and Parmesan.

NOTE: After step 1, you can transfer the mixture to a blender or use a handheld blender to purée. I don't usually bother with this, but Henry has a lifelong aversion to "ucky slimy bits" (cooked garlic, onion, celery, etc.) and prefers his sauces smooth. I must admit that blending produces a pretty color and nice texture, but this dish is delicious either way.

Jonah's Guacamole

Serves as many people as you want it to

Tomatoes, fresh cilantro, onion, and jalapeño, to taste
Avocados (1 for every 2 people)
Fresh lemon juice, to taste (lime juice is also good)
Salt, to taste

1. In a bowl, chop the tomatoes, cilantro, onion, and jalapeño. Add avocado, lime juice, and salt until it tastes really good.

Poblano, Roasted Corn, and White Bean Chili

Serves 6–8

4 poblano peppers

¼ cup olive oil, plus more for rubbing

1 pound small white navy beans, sorted, soaked at least 4 hours, rinsed, and drained

4 medium ears corn (in husks)

1 medium onion, thinly sliced

4 cloves garlic, chopped

1 tablespoon dried oregano

2 teaspoons ground cumin

1 teaspoon plus pinch salt, divided

Big handful fresh cilantro leaves, divided

2 tablespoons fresh lime juice

Big handful raw pumpkin seeds

2 tablespoons whole milk

8 ounces soft goat cheese

1. Preheat the oven to 425°F.

2. Rub the poblanos lightly with oil and place on a baking sheet. Roast for 30 to 45 minutes, turning occasionally, until charred on all sides.

3. While poblanos are roasting, place the beans in a large pot with 6 cups of cold water. Bring to a boil, cover, reduce to a strong simmer, and cook 1 hour or so, until the beans are tender but not mushy. Check regularly to make sure beans are immersed in water—add more if necessary. When done cooking, remove from the heat and set aside.

RECIPE CONTINUES

4. When the poblanos are roasted, transfer them to a medium bowl, cover tightly with plastic wrap, and let steam for 15 minutes. Rub off the skins as best you can. Roughly chop and set aside. Reduce the oven heat to 350°F.

5. Roast the corn (keep the husks on) for 30 minutes. When it's cool enough to handle, husk the corn, and, using a sharp knife, scrape off the kernels. Discard the husks, set the kernels aside in a bowl.

6. In a large pot over medium heat, warm the olive oil. Add the onion and a small pinch of salt. When the onions sizzle, reduce the heat to low and cook 10 minutes, stirring occasionally. Add the garlic, oregano, cumin, salt, about half of the cilantro leaves, and the chopped poblanos. Cook for 5 minutes, stirring occasionally.

7. Scrape every bit of the onion mixture into a blender. Scoop out ½ cup or so of the bean cooking liquid and add to blender. Blend well, at least 1 minute. You will have a gorgeous green saucy paste. It will smell so good you won't believe it. Add more liquid, if necessary, to get to the consistency of pesto. Stir the mixture into the beans.

8. Add the corn and lime juice to the beans. Taste and adjust the seasoning as needed. Over low heat, simmer for 15 minutes. Stir occasionally to ensure beans don't stick or burn. You might need to add a little more water if it starts to dry out. Keep covered until ready to serve.

9. Meanwhile, in a medium skillet over medium-high heat, roast the pumpkin seeds. Stir constantly for 4 to 5 minutes, until the seeds pop and smell toasty. This demands constant attention. They will turn on you and burn in a second. Remove from the heat and set aside.

10. In a small saucepan over medium-low heat, warm the milk. Add the goat cheese and stir constantly for 1 to 2 minutes to make a smooth sauce.

11. To serve, ladle chili into each individual bowl. Spoon a few tablespoons of goat-cheese sauce on top. Garnish with pumpkin seeds and the remaining cilantro.

ACKNOWLEDGMENTS

Many thanks to:

Doug Seibold at Agate for making it happen and making it better.

Also at Agate: Danielle McLimore, Jessica Easto, Eileen Johnson, Zachary Rudin, Morgan Krehbiel, and Deirdre Kennedy.

My stellar team of recipe testers: Robbie Fulks, Gerald Dowd, Amanda Burness Dowd, Justin Roberts, Juliana Hatfield, Catie May, Alex May, Michelle Yamada, Frank Yamada, Jimmy Johnson, Pam Kasper, Len Kasper, Jennifer Schacker, Brian Bouldrey, Catherine Carrigan, Emily Steadman, Jason Narducy, and Lauren MacIntyre.

My agent, Jenni Ferrari-Adler, for saying yes at the right time.

Rochelle Bourgault for bringing the book back to life, and for the title.

My writing teachers and mentors, especially Anthony Cropper, Robert Gundlach, David Belbin, and Graham Joyce.

My fellow travellers in writing, especially Jez Noond, Charles Harmon, Lauren MacIntyre, Lauren Stacks, and Jennifer Schacker, many of whom read early drafts of the manuscript and improved it more than I could have on my own.

Brian Bouldrey, for being a great teacher, colleague, and friend, and for braving it through the entire first draft.

Rebecca Dudley for technical support, moral support, photographs, and walks by the lake.

Joshua Chambers-Letson for comradeship when I needed it badly, and for letting me use his phone.

Dale Lawrence for always knowing the best places to eat.

Scott Pack, Matt Weiland, and Jason Narducy for good advice.

John Strohm for so many things, especially his sharp memory and swift fact-checking.

Steven Hillage for the Rainbow Dome Musick that soothed and spurred me through a difficult second draft.

Friends who inspired, encouraged, and supported this project, especially Michael Latham (AKA Jacob's dad) and Jeanne-Marie Greiner.

Ira Robbins, Juliana Hatfield, Tanya Donelly, Bill Janowitz, Anthony DeCurtis, Len Kasper, Chrissie Dickinson, Bill Wyman, and Stacee Sledge.

Nathan Walker at Riot Act Media.

My parents and in-laws, all.

Zirque for soup, generosity, and inspiration.

Lulu for the amazing chocolate that fueled my editing.

Jake for being a nasty bass player, a willing dishwasher, a crack editor, and my favorite person to feed.

Henry. For Pop Pie, pesto, and for keeping me on my toes every single day.

Most of all, Jonah: From Buddha baby to beardy bookworm, you make life look easy and have taught me to lighten up since the moment you were born. Thank you for being game. Keep cooking!

RECIPE INDEX

Vegan Strawberry–Cream Scones 13

White Whole-Wheat Bread 15

Roast Chicken and Vegetables 34

Chicken Noodle Soup 36

Meatloaf with Mashed-Potato Topping 38

New York Strip 40

Spicy Hummus 55

Red Pepper–Cashew Spread 56

Tempeh Mock-Chicken Salad 57

Spinach and White Bean Stew 58

Vegetarian Baked Beans 59

Vegetarian Refried Bean Burritos 60

Lentils and Caramelized Onions with Capellini 62

Sweet and Spicy Vermicelli Stir-Fry 73

Mushroom and Kale Stir-Fry 75

Greens with Peanut–Ginger Sauce 77

Macaroni and Cheese.. 92

Butternut Squash Ziti 94

Tempeh Tetrazzini... 96

Blueberry Pie 99

Potatoes au Gratin.. 110

Fish in a Pouch 111

Stuffed Portobello Mushrooms... 113

Mushroom Enchiladas with Roasted Red Pepper and
    Tomato Sauce 115

Mung Bean Soup.. 129

Zirque's Split Pea and Squash Soup 131

Condo Pad Black Bean Soup 133

New England Clam Chowder 134

Yellow Cake with Chocolate Frosting................................ 143

Vegan Banana Cupcakes with Vegan Cream Cheese Frosting.............145

Vegan Ginger–Carrot Cake with Maple–Orange Glaze........................147

Chocolate–Raspberry Cupcakes 149

Hijiki with Tempeh.. 166

Strawberry–Banana Smoothie 168

Raw Slaw with Creamy Pine Nut Dressing....................... 169

Peanut Butter and Miso Ramen Soup................................. 170

Zirque's Vegan Chocolate Ice-Cream Balls 172

Spinach and Brazil Nut Pesto 181

Vegan Basil Miso Pesto 181

Pistachio Hot Pepper Pesto 182

Garlic Placenta 183

Vegetarian Biscuits and Gravy 191

Fried Green Tomatoes 193

Maple–Peanut–Cacao Granola 194

The Cosmic Muffin 195

Eggs Ahmet 204

Sherried Mushroom Omelet 205

Pasta Fagioli 215

Jonah's Guacamole 216

Poblano, Roasted Corn, and White Bean Chili 217

ABOUT THE AUTHOR

FREDA LOVE SMITH is a lecturer in the School of Communication at Northwestern University. She is the co-founder of the bands the Mysteries of Life and the Blake Babies, who were regulars on MTV and critically applauded in *The Village Voice, Rolling Stone*, and *Spin*. She has a monthly column in *Paste* and her short stories have appeared in journals such as *The North American Review, Smokelong, Bound Off*, and *Riptide*. She lives in Evanston, Illinois, with her partner, Jake Smith, and son Henry.